Why Men Won't Commit

Why Men Won't Commit

GETTING WHAT YOU BOTH WANT WITHOUT PLAYING GAMES

GEORGE WEINBERG, Ph.D.

ATRIA BOOKS

New York London Toronto Sydney Singapore

ATRIA BOOKS

1230 Avenue of the Americas
New York, NY 10020

ISBN: 0-7434-4569-4

First Atria Books hardcover printing February 2003

10   9   8   7   6   5   4   3   2   1

ATRIA BOOKS is a trademark of Simon & Schuster, Inc.

For information regarding special discounts for bulk purchases,
please contact Simon & Schuster Special Sales at 1-800-456-6798 or
business@simonandschuster.com

Designed by Helene Berinsky

Printed in the U.S.A.

What is life when wanting love?
Night without a morning

—ROBERT BURNS

Acknowledgments

A number of people made this book possible. Chief among them were Dianne Rowe, whose astute sense of the English language and knowledge of people kept the manuscript on track at every stage; Barbara Lowenstein, my friend and agent, who conceived of the book and made suggestions all along the way; Kim Meisner, my editor, who amended the final version. Her suggestions added kindness and an overall sensitivity to the whole project. Others whose counsel during the writing was extremely helpful were Lawrence Abrams, Lauren Howard, and Patrice Robertie.

Contents

PART THREE
Taking Care of Yourself

Introduction

Wherever you turn, from lunch tables to sitcoms, you hear women talking about men as being irrational, infantile, and afraid of commitment. Men play into this image by acting as if marriage is a trap, by looking scared if a woman mentions the future, and by being notoriously afraid to say "I love you."

You may have experienced the problem yourself. You may be attractive, bright, capable, articulate, and ready to love. More than once, you may have thought that the man in your life was great for you, only to realize that he wasn't going ahead another step. You tried different approaches, but after a while you felt shaken, and it was hard to do anything right. You got angry at yourself and very angry at him. Maybe your man ended the relationship, maybe you did. But either way, now it's over, and you're still not sure exactly why.

Obviously you don't want this to happen in your next relationship, which may have already started. Yet you can't help worrying. Even if there is real love on both sides, you know from experience

(not just from yours but from those of your women friends) how easily things can go wrong. Men have a way of pulling back suddenly.

It may seem that you've been facing men's classic problem—
commitmentphobia—that men just don't want relationships the
way women do. But this is oversimple and not true. **Men actually
want commitment, love, and permanence every bit as much as
women do.**

So why do many men act as if they don't?

What terrifies men in love relationships isn't commitment but
what they perceive as **the loss of their masculinity**—the strange way
that they view masculinity. The secret of why men won't commit
(even when they *want* to) involves very particular fears that nearly
all men have. Without realizing it, you may risk triggering your
man's fear by simple acts that can make him afraid to commit to you
for life.

From childhood, men have been brought up to be strong and
silent—never to show weakness. They've been taught that to say
they're afraid, or in pain, or even that they're happy or in love is
unmanly. Most men have spent so many years putting their feelings
aside that by adulthood they lose their ability to describe many of
their feelings, or even to know what they are. But they still have feelings, of course—which become unidentified forces within them
that confuse them. What we can't identify always feels very exaggerated, and most men react in exaggerated ways when they're
bewildered and threatened.

The feelings that confuse men the most and often lead them to
act in dramatic ways are *feelings of threat to their masculinity.* It's
these feelings that stop them from commitment. Your man has the
tremendous (and largely unnecessary) burden of having to maintain
a masculine image, which he feels can be very easily put in
jeopardy—especially by a woman whom he loves.

*   *   *

The worst mistake that women make in relationships is to *overestimate* men. Men pretend to be in control, to know what they're doing. But men aren't nearly as secure as they would have you believe. Men don't have the insight into their emotions that women do. Real insight takes courage. When we first look inside of ourselves, we don't always like what we see. So most men don't bother to look.

Your man is probably worried about aspects of his own self-presentation that might seem utterly trivial to you. He feels threats that you can't possibly even imagine, but he can't talk about them. If he could, he would probably see that he wasn't under threat at all. The two of you could discuss things and put them in perspective. You could help him see that commitment to you would pose no threat to his masculine image.

But because the threat remains at the level of a vague feeling—what I call a gut reaction—it can ruin everything. Your man is too much ruled by his gut reactions, and when his gut reactions are bad, he wants to run away. He may overreact to small things that bother him in your relationship because he has no idea what to say or do to make things better. Unfortunately, this means that the man in your life is likely to make big decisions about you—decisions often based on fear, like the fear of being trapped or the fear of showing softness—without knowing why.

Most men are on a quest for the ready-made perfect woman because they basically feel that problems in a relationship *can't be worked out*. When the slightest thing goes wrong, it seems easier to bolt than to talk.

The man you began dating last week, or whom you've been going with for six months, has gut reactions to you aplenty. Most of them are positive, or he wouldn't be with you. But he may also have certain negative reactions that stop him from committing himself to you. He has been afraid to look inside himself for such a long time that he couldn't tell you what they are, even under truth serum. But *you* can know what they are.

This book is about why men won't commit. But more specifically, it's about what you can do to help your man overcome his irrational fears so that he can commit himself to you fully. As a woman, you probably have an insight into feelings that most men don't. Feelings have been an integral part of your life. You have lived with yours, talked to your friends about them, and accepted them as a part of you. You have used your awareness of your feelings to improve past relationships. Now you can use your knowledge to improve this relationship, easily and at no cost to yourself. You can help your man move toward the commitment that he secretly craves.

Men are much more alike than they seem to be. Nearly any man who likes you and wants a relationship to grow will look for basically the same treatment from you.

True, this new man in your life may seem very different from the last one. Men's personalities have been shaped by family histories, their interests, their skills, and so forth. But these account for only surface differences. **All men's basic psychological needs are the same, and these needs determine their gut reactions.** You can go from one man to the next, but if you continue acting in the same ways, you will predictably get basically the same responses, good or bad.

Obviously, some things you can't help. If a man's gut reaction to you is wrong in a way that you can't control, it's time to move on before you get in too deep. Maybe you simply don't appeal to him enough, for whatever reason. You're too far apart in life goals, or you're the wrong religion. Or it's physical—you're too tall, or you're a blonde, and he likes dark women. In these cases, so be it. It's time to move on.

On the other hand, the problem might be rooted in something that can be changed. For example, you're the same height as your man, but you always wear heels. And he never says, "Please don't wear those three-inch stilettos." That would be a shame if you might have been very happy together. You may ask now, "Why didn't he simply tell me? He mattered more to me than my choice of shoes." He probably didn't tell you because he just "felt bad," and he himself didn't understand why. He felt some vague threat to his masculinity. But he didn't stop to analyze his feelings or your attire. It was easier to withdraw and perhaps find a woman who made him feel big and strong. The perfect ready-made woman!

Your man may react this way to other things you do that make him feel threatened. He feels somewhat upset by something that you are doing, perhaps innocently, but fails to bring it up, and so you go on doing it. Many tragedies in relationships occur when the woman creates bad reactions by behavior that she would willingly change, and might even prefer to change.

Sometimes you can make a critical difference in a relationship just by understanding what is going on in your man's mind. Too often women think that in order to keep a man, they have to make major sacrifices. They betray their own basic needs, trying to remold themselves out of desperation. As things get more hopeless, they may stop taking care of themselves altogether. Your man can't always talk to you about what's bothering him, but if you can figure out what he's really irrationally afraid of, you can make tiny adjustments early so that you won't be tempted to make big ones later on.

Take the case of my patient Richard. He met Tracy at a film festival, and they connected wonderfully right from the start. Richard was a schoolteacher, and Tracy was a successful travel agent. Richard was extremely attracted to Tracy and was excited to have found someone who shared his interest in books and in old films. Their first few dates went very well. Neither of them said much about their first marriages.

But on their fourth date, they started talking about the locations of some of their favorite movies. Tracy mentioned that she had made a point of using her travel connections to visit some of the famous locations with her husband. She got very animated when she described how "Bob and I went to Venice and Monaco, and even Algiers." She described Bob as a competent traveler. "One thing you have to say about Bob. He was a fearless driver. You should have seen him on those narrow roads in Monaco."

Richard got unusually quiet, but Tracy didn't notice. It never occurred to her that Richard was reacting badly, that he had no desire to see Bob driving fearlessly with Tracy at his side in Monaco. The conversation shifted, and the topic seemed to be closed. But Richard went home with a very bad gut reaction, which he didn't even want to think about. The next week in my office Richard told me that he really liked Tracy, but that he was thinking of winding down the relationship. He said that it just didn't feel right to him. Observing the radical change in his picture of Tracy, I questioned Richard and finally elicited the memory of that conversation about Tracy's ex-husband and all the fun that she'd had with him. Once I got Richard to put into words what was bothering him, he was able to discuss it with Tracy.

At my prompting, Richard told Tracy that the conversation had pained him. He had felt that Tracy was setting him up against her ex-husband. He had felt unmanned in what he interpreted as a competition with her ex-husband. He'd had the irrational feeling that Tracy was being disloyal to him.

Tracy was amazed. She'd had no intention of conveying anything like that. She told Richard that she had never been as attracted to her ex-husband as she was to him, and that they'd had very little in common. By the time they had gone to Europe, their marriage was already in serious trouble, and in Europe all they had done was fight.

Because Richard was able to identify his gut reaction and tell Tracy how upset he'd been, Tracy was able to explain what she had really meant. Tracy had never imagined that Richard would see her as being disloyal or emasculating if she praised her ex-husband's driving. After all, she was with Richard now and not with him. *She* knew that much of her marriage had been miserable. She could barely stand to talk to her ex-husband these days.

But Richard's need for loyalty was very strong and irrationally intense. And his reaction to perceived disloyalty was well over the top. Once Tracy knew about this oversensitivity, she could deal with it easily and establish her loyalty early.

After a while, Tracy got the whole loyalty issue out of the way. As Richard's positive gut reactions grew, he stopped evaluating Tracy and came to accept her as the terrific person she really was. Soon Richard was the one pushing for commitment. His need for loyalty actually began working in Tracy's favor.

Are men's gut reactions justified? In many cases no. But as they say, life isn't fair. Richard was extremely tough on Tracy for what was actually a totally innocent comment. He was tough because he didn't know what he was feeling. He didn't identify his irrational feeling of threat. As I mentioned, when we don't know what we're feeling, we tend to overreact.

Like Richard, many man have profound gut reactions. Because they are unable to put them into words, these reactions may rule them in a very negative way. When you know what's bothering you, you can deal with it. But if you don't know what's wrong, it eats at you.

Because men are so often in the dark in relationships, they tend to overreact to imperfections and pull back when they really want to come forward. So long as you, yourself, are not also in the dark, you can help your man and help yourself by making commitment easier.

The key is to understand men's secret concerns, and in particular those of the primary man in your life. When you do understand them, you can make them work to your advantage.

You certainly won't have to spend a lifetime studying the man you're with. No relationship would be worth that. And of course no relationship is worth the constant burden of your having to play games to keep it going.

Many women, feeling hopeless about their man's seeming inability to commit, resort to game playing—like making him jealous or acting hard to get—as ways of overcoming the resistance that they meet. But all calculated devices designed to overcome "men's fear of commitment" eventually result in a war between the sexes. Men have a powerful radar that tells them to run away when anyone tries to "overcome" them, when any strategy is being used on them.

Once you understand that your man wants commitment just as much as you do, you won't feel the need to play games. You will be free of "the battle of the sexes" mentality.

The art of sustaining a love affair is for two people to learn each other's sensitivities early on, so that there aren't major surprises as the relationship progresses. Once you do that, you will be able to give and to get what you both want in the relationship. After a while, you will be having a wonderful and effortless time with your man. You will enjoy a lasting love affair and get what you need as well.

As you start thinking about men's gut reactions, they may seem frighteningly random, like land mines hidden on your path to happiness with a man. When you trigger one accidentally, trouble ensues and the man pulls back. But, fortunately, things aren't really random at all.

Men's gut reactions fall into four basic categories, which spring from four special psychological needs that all men share. If not met, each of these needs prompts your man to feel threatened in particular ways. These needs are basic to his sense of masculinity. No matter how old a man is, how experienced, how sophisticated—he will have these needs. Every man does.

All men have:

(1) the need to be special
(2) the need to travel light
(3) the need for loyalty, and
(4) the need to be close emotionally.

These needs are easily stated and may sound familiar, but once you understand how the male psyche works, you will see that they are anything but simple. Each need takes very subtle forms and runs deep. In some men, one need is more dominant than the others. But all men have these four needs.

Your man's readiness to commit reflects how you, as a woman, deal with these four basic needs.

In this book, we will encounter men's four basic needs again and again. We will see how these needs are basic to men's feelings of masculinity. They give rise to the gut reactions that make or break your future with a man. To understand these needs is to gain real control. If you do this in a direct and honest way, you can turn possible trouble into an opportunity to bond better than ever with the man you want.

We will also discuss what I call the Masculine Pretense, the set of attitudes that men imagine defines their masculinity. It's these attitudes that cause your man to feel so threatened and make it hard for him to commit.

MY OWN VANTAGE POINT

I am a psychotherapist, and I've been in private practice a long time. During the last ten years, I've been working mostly with men. This makes my practice quite unusual, since the majority of people in therapy are women. As everyone knows, women are more ready than men to talk about themselves and to explore what is going on in their lives.

Nearly all the men who come to me are outwardly successful. Many of them have their own businesses, or are professionals, or creative artists, and at the very least they are aspiring and enterprising. But when it comes to their love life, it's a different story. They unconsciously want that part of their life to take care of itself, and of course it doesn't.

Very few of the men I work with start therapy by talking about relationships. They usually begin by talking about what they're good at—like making money, handling people, keeping a number of irons in the fire. They pride themselves on their power and efficiency, or on the fact that others depend on them. Only slowly does it come out that these men are deeply concerned about relationships, either one that they are in, or one that they are considering, or a marriage that is on the rocks and that they don't know how to save. Many blame themselves for their failures. ("I work too hard." "I travel too much.") Though some have gone through many relationships, they still have very little insight. "I guess I'm just no good with women."

All feel lonely—as lonely as my women patients have felt over the years. The difference is that it takes the men a lot longer to admit to themselves that they feel disappointed and alone. In fact, I often have to question them at length about their feelings before they tell me this.

After talking to hundreds of men who finally opened up to me, I am convinced that men want relationships just as much as women do.

They don't see themselves as being phobic about commitment. On the contrary, they are deeply disappointed when they lose a possible soul mate, even if they are the ones who ended the relationship.

Many of these men feel that a promise of life was broken to them. "What promise?" I ask. Nearly all tell me that they dreamed of being with a woman, not just a woman attractive to them, but one who is loving, loyal, spiritual, truly with them for better or for worse. They find plenty of attractive women, they tell me, and an abundance of available women. But it just never works out.

These men usually describe at least one relationship that looked perfect for a time before it collapsed. Usually the man has simply withdrawn. The woman panicked, not knowing why she was losing him. Ironically, the man usually couldn't say either.

In studying male-female relationships, I have become increasingly aware of the fragility of men's egos. The failure to realize that even the most seemingly successful men are, deep inside, unsure of themselves has led women with the best of intentions into difficulties that they have not understood. By failing to appreciate what men really need, they have elicited bad gut reactions—sometimes fatal to the relationship—when by doing *less*, they could have taken better care of themselves and kept the relationship heading in the direction they wanted it to go.

Recently, I came in at what felt like the tail end of a great but short love affair, full of good sex and good times, where everything had seemed right. Greg had built his own recruitment agency from the bottom up. Just about the time he met Jennifer, his business started to take off. Greg talked excitedly to Jennifer about expanding and improving his operation. Jennifer jumped right in. Trying to make herself useful to Greg, she devoted herself to seeing places for possible improvement. Hardly a day went by without her suggesting something for his business.

But while Jennifer imagined that she was helping Greg, he began feeling worse and worse. He was having a very bad gut reaction to Jennifer, and he had no idea why. They came to me in a last-ditch attempt to recover their relationship. I could see that Greg was responding to Jennifer's suggestions in two ways. He was delighted with her involvement, and she had some good ideas, but she was so prolific in her efforts to help him that he began to feel like a failure. He felt that Jennifer no longer saw him as he really was—a man who had succeeded because of his own merits and who was on the verge of a great adventure.

Jennifer had actually put him up too high. She saw him as so successful and sure of himself that he was above being hurt by anything she said. In her haste to help Greg, Jennifer had unknowingly denied Greg's need to be seen as an individual—in the way *he* wanted to be seen, as an accomplished person.

At my advice, Jennifer offered Greg no further suggestions for improvement for two months, and after that only sparingly. When she saw anything good, she complimented Greg, as she had when they'd first met. Greg's gut reaction changed for the better almost at once. Greg once again saw Jennifer as the supportive, giving person that she was, and they are still together.

The man in your life is acutely reactive, both positively and negatively, to small acts of yours. He has much stronger gut reactions to you, both good and bad, than he lets on. If he is like nearly all men, he likes to pretend to himself, and to you, that he is above these gut reactions, but he isn't.

If your man cares for you at all, you are much more important to him than you realize. *And he is more subject to your influence than you realize.* This is double-edged. True you risk bad gut reactions. But with understanding, you can create the gut reactions that lead to commitment.

PART ONE

His Basic Needs

Men Are the Weaker Sex

If you eavesdropped on women telling their relationship stories to psychotherapists in offices across the country, you would think that it was woman's role to suffer, to hope, and to hang on. And that it was a man's role to be strong and to make his decisions about the woman in his life as slowly as he can. You wonder, "Will he see me a second time?" "Will he introduce me to his friends or family?" "Will he ever decide to marry me?"

You may question his commitment to you even more than whether you want to go ahead with him. For instance, you worry that he'll tire of you sexually, but not that you will tire of him or find him inadequate and not worth your time. You see him as holding all the cards.

If this is your perception, you are almost surely in for trouble. You may see every day that you stay together and maybe every time he calls you as a victory. But you are sacrificing too much, struggling too hard for what should be yours automatically in a love affair. If you see this man as your last chance, things will work out badly whether you continue together or not. You will be in so much pain, and so angry at him for having power over you, that you may actually end up happier if he leaves you.

Here's the irony. He doesn't hold all the cards. He is just pretending to. **If you can realize the truth, that men are the weaker sex, you will have ten times the chance in your relationship.** The man in your life isn't nearly as strong as he looks. He may try to make even his romantic decisions look rational, as if he is dealing from strength. But what you are seeing is only his Masculine Pretense, not his real self.

The Masculine Pretense consists of a set of attitudes that your man feels he must show to the world in order to be a man. It is the pose that he is strong, independent, free, and in control. It includes the idea that other people can't hurt him emotionally, and that people can't move him deeply. To the extent that your man buys into this pretense, he behaves as if he doesn't need you or anyone else the way you need him. Of course, the Masculine Pretense is merely that—a pretense. Underneath this pretense, your man is as afraid of being alone, as subject to pain and pleasure, and as much in need of love as you are. In his heart, he knows that he isn't dealing from strength at all.

Because he doesn't allow himself to see the truth, his responses bespeak confusion rather than clarity, and his relationship with you is more bewildering to him than it is to you. Even if your man loves being with you, he is less clear than you are about what moves him toward you or away from you. He is ruled by gut reactions, which he himself can't put into words. In this respect, he is probably quite undeveloped compared to you and your close women friends. He doesn't know exactly why he loves you or why he chose you over everyone else.

And if he gets upset, if something goes off course in the relationship, he won't be clear on what to do about it. He may be quick to give up rather than try to set things right. Because your man is more in the dark than you are about his emotions, he is more ruled by his gut reactions.

Sally was a first-year graduate student, and Tom was a full-time tenured instructor at the same midwestern university. He met her at a campus Christmas party. Tom had the reputation of being a young genius, and Sally had intended to take one of his courses the next year. When they met, she was enthralled by Tom's education and wisdom, and by his knowledge of her field, French literature. She was stunned by her instant attraction to him, and she was delighted when he asked her out. Their relationship began with the kind of romance that teacher-student relationships often lead to. Making love began as a conspiracy to break the barriers.

Right from the start, Sally sensed that Tom liked being an authority, the man with the answers. He made suggestions for all of her papers; he offered to look at whatever she was working on. One weekend, he insisted on spending a day and a half fixing her computer, instead of working on the book that he hoped would establish him in his field.

Actually, Sally didn't need the help at all. She was a scholarship student who had always gotten straight A's on her own. She accepted Tom's help because it felt sexy; it made her feel closer to him. After a few months, however, Tom's attitude toward Sally suddenly changed. He often became nasty and irritable with her, seemingly for no reason, sometimes in front of other people. Sally tried to talk to Tom about it, but he just told her that he was sick of "doing everything for her." The second time Sally returned to her apartment in tears after Tom had insulted her at a party, she ended the relationship.

Sally had no idea that Tom was having a very bad gut reaction to her that he couldn't put into words. Tom hadn't told Sally about his uneasiness when he started to overdose on his role of being the "answer man." He hadn't even understood the problem himself. He had gone from seeing Sally as his inspiration to resenting her and feeling that she was stealing something precious from him. He had dreams that she was stopping him from writing the book that would put him on the map.

Tom started in therapy with me soon after the breakup with Sally. He had been calling to see her again, but she refused. In therapy, I helped Tom to see that his relationship with Sally wasn't the first time he had lost something good because of a bad gut reaction. Tom had felt used by women before. In fact, it had become a repetitive pattern for him. When he first met a woman, Tom's Masculine Pretense would take over, and he would show off by helping the woman and impressing her with his vast knowledge. Soon, he would start to resent the woman, and before either of them knew what was happening, the relationship went down in flames. Tom was brilliant in some respects, but like many men, he had almost no sense of what he was feeling or why. Only when a feeling became very intense did it get his attention, and by then it was always too late. With all his academic genius, his gut reactions were acute and very primitive. If Sally had understood more about men's gut reactions, she might have been the woman to end the vicious cycle and get Tom to commit. They could have made a great team.

Like all men, Tom had the need to travel light. If Sally had understood this need, she could have insisted that he not do too much for her. She would have protected her own dignity, improved his gut reaction to her, and saved the relationship.

Of course, much of Sally's problem came from Tom's problem. But you are going to run into men with problems, including the kind that Tom had. And among those men are very decent ones, who suffer as much from losing you as you do from losing them.

The man in your life may be pulling back these days, even if he needs you every bit as much as you need him—or more. Needing you is one thing. *Knowing that he needs you* is another. Most men are very poor at knowing what they need emotionally. This is why you need to understand their gut reactions as well as you can.

HOW THEIR MASCULINE PRETENSE GETS MEN IN TROUBLE

Speaking for men generally, let me say that it isn't strictly our fault that we tend to be in the dark about many of our true feelings. We have been limited by our Masculine Pretense—a pretense that has been imposed upon us since childhood. During childhood we were trained for worldly success, which required being rational and forceful. We would become athletes or businessmen, or professionals at something. We were not encouraged to know ourselves emotionally. In fact, we were taught that feelings get in the way.

Think about the emotional straitjacket that we men have been placed in. You as a girl were permitted to be indecisive or frightened. If you truly had no experience at something, you were allowed to look inexperienced. If someone's criticism hurt, you could say so. You could cry if you felt like it. If someone didn't invite you to a party and you felt bad, you could show it on your face. If someone complimented you, you could glow. You were encouraged to be emotive. As a woman, you were expected to feel things deeply. During those same early years, the man in your life was being sent in a very different direction. His goal was to become strong, independent, not needy. He was taught not to show emotion, to discount his feelings and "get on with it," to do what had to be done without ever letting joy or dismay absorb him. Over time, you developed your interest in feelings and in other people. By your teens, you very likely stopped discussing the ups and downs of every social exchange with your mother, even if you did do this as a girl.

You substituted peers and, women friends for her back then and continued to over the years.

To this very day, you can talk with one or two close women friends about a date or even a sexual relationship. You can get on the phone and ask for their opinions about what to wear, or what a man meant when he said something in particular to you. You can ask for advice about what to say if a man calls and about what to do if he doesn't. You don't mind showing anxiety if you feel it.

During those same developmental years, when you were learning to talk things out, the man in your life was learning not to be sidetracked by feelings and not to express them. Although his life was replete with challenges, how he felt about those challenges seemed beside the point. Discouraged from discussing his emotions with other people, he grew lonelier. He actually lost the ability to talk about his deepest feelings, to know what they are. Today, even if he has good male friends, it's unlikely that he tells them about the ups and downs of his emotional relationships. These friends probably have little or no idea of what's really going on between him and you.

For instance, suppose you had a big fight with him and almost broke up a few nights ago. It ended well, you made love, but the misunderstanding remains like a fault line that you fear can result in another earthquake and maybe a final break between you. You discussed the quarrel with a close woman friend, recalling as much as you could of what you said and what he said. Your friend offered you her best opinion about where it was your fault and where it was his. She suggested corrections or perhaps recommended an apology. Or maybe she told you to stick to your guns, that you were completely right. Most important, she propped you up, and you know that you will have her in your life even if the relationship with your man ends badly.

Your lover is at the ball game today with his two best men

friends. But he probably won't even mention the argument. If asked how things are going with you, he may say with affected casualness, "Fine." He almost feels it as a point of honor not to discuss intimate matters with anyone else. Silence is part of his Masculine Pretense. Very likely, he still feels shaken by the trouble he had with you. He may feel even more devastated and alone than you do because he has fewer confidants than you have. You can say to a woman friend, "I very much want this relationship to work. I hope that it does." He hesitates to admit even this much. Because of his Masculine Pretense, he censors himself utterly. Compared with him, you are uncensored.

It's the same with your man's positive feelings. He is weak when it comes to expressing them too. Love wants to declare itself—to be seen by others. You can indulge these impulses. After spending a wonderful weekend with him, you eagerly call a woman friend and describe the experience: "It was wonderful, the best weekend of my life. He was tender and affectionate. we made some plans, and we started talking about staying together." On the other hand, his Masculine Pretense stops him from celebrating the same experience. He's probably afraid to admit even to himself that the weekend was as good as it really was. If he talks about it at all, the most he may say is that the sex was good and that he plans to keep seeing you.

The man in your life has all the same emotions that you have, down deep. But because of his Masculine Pretense, he won't let on how he feels. And not letting on has become a habit for him. He doesn't let on even to himself, as he should. Because of this weakness, he will be baffled by small setbacks in his relationship with you. When there is trouble with you, he won't understand it, or why he feels so defeated, why it appears to him that he lost so much. No matter how much he may rant about what he thinks you are doing wrong, he is often stricken and confused.

Not only his emotions, but also the basic reasons why he needs you remain a mystery to him. What we can't say to others over years, we tend to stop saying to ourselves. And so, over time, he has lost his power of analysis—of identifying what is really going on in his romance with you. Although you have delved into relationships, perhaps enough to be an expert about them, he probably hasn't. Even if he has had many relationships, he may well be a beginner when it comes to emotional understanding. You are probably reading this book to get a deeper insight into your relationship. This week, he is more likely to be reading a spy novel or a book on golf than a book on relationships. Because your man doesn't process his feelings or understand them the way you do, he has only his gut reactions to go on.

THE FOUR BASIC NEEDS THAT ALL MEN HAVE

Though relationships may appear to be quite different, all men have basically the same four needs, and you need to know about them. Even though your man is unique and your relationship is special, he has these needs just like every other man. He feels them intensely because of his Masculine Pretense. These needs, which determine his gut reactions to you at every stage of a relationship, take different forms as you grow closer. As a romance progresses, they evolve, develop, and change. If you attend to these needs early, love and trust will grow rapidly. Though he will always have these needs in some form, they won't be so volatile after the first six months.

1. **His need to be recognized as special.** This means being appreciated not just as "a man" but also in a personal way. You would do well to think about this need, especially when you first meet a new man but of course later on too. As a gut reaction,

this man will judge you right away by how much individuality he has to you, how different from all other men you make him feel. As time goes by, this need of his will assume other forms, as all his needs will. But if you don't deal with it early on, there won't be a "later on."

2. His need to travel light. This springs from an irrational fear of being encumbered. You may have a little of this fear yourself, but you probably aren't nearly as paranoid as most men are about being limited or tied down. As a relationship progresses, this need becomes more pronounced. From childhood, your man has identified "growing up and being a real man" with the absolute right to control his own time, money, and decisions about where he goes and with whom. A serious fear of his is that commitment will require him to surrender all his "hard-won" masculine freedoms. He needs to understand that committing to you does not mean emasculation or imprisonment. You can reassure him that it's safe to move forward with you, and that, even with marriage and a family, he can still travel light and be free—within reason, of course.

3. His need for loyalty. This is one that you certainly understand and share. But because you are more in touch with this need than your man is and aren't ashamed of it, you deal with it better. The fact is, your man is probably far more terrified of being betrayed than you are. Because of his Masculine Pretense, he feels that he has to be in control to prove that he is a man. The idea of "his" woman not being completely on his side unmans him. Most men fear betrayal even when it isn't happening.

4. His need to be close emotionally. His need for this is exactly like yours, so much so that your man may view it as a kind of problem—as a blemish on his masculinity. This need looks like a weakness to him, a quality that makes him more female than male. Of course, we know that this isn't so. But his perception can mean trouble for you. Here too the Masculine Pretense is rearing its head and complicating things. It's easy for you to admit that you want intimacy, that you want affection and closeness from him. He wants to be close emotionally just as much as you do. But he finds it hard, if not impossible, to say so. More likely, like someone emerging from a desert and dying of thirst, he will simply gulp it down like water when he gets it. But he will also be deeply hurt when he feels that closeness is missing.

Just remember that like you, your man is accomplished in some ways but uncertain in others. Above all, he is not a god, and he knows it. At best, he is a forceful, responsible, caring person, with plenty on his plate. He is not a finished product, but a man in the process of creating himself and discovering himself. If things go right, you will help him in this process. At best, you will validate him in the ways that count most, and he will do the same for you.

Let's look at a man's four basic needs. You will see how understanding them can help you create the gut reactions in your man that lead to commitment.

2

See Me As I Really Am, Not Only As I Pretend to Be

YOUR MAN'S FIRST BASIC NEED
—THE CRAVING TO BE SPECIAL

You've just been introduced to a good-looking new man. You wonder what he thinks of you. You want him to see you as sexy, stylish, and bright. It's human nature to try to come across as well as you can. In the beginning of any relationship, you will find yourself thinking overtime about the impression that you are making. Are you attractive enough, educated enough, from a good enough family? If things go well, you won't worry so much later on. But it's only natural to start out wanting to put your best foot forward. Most of the books and articles that you've read on dating stress this almost exclusively—how you can arrange to be seen in the best possible light.

This all makes sense as far as it goes. But it doesn't go far enough. It overestimates half of the equation and neglects the all-important other half. How this man sees you is very important, of course. But starting right away, he is also forming a sense of *how you see him* and of whether you see him at all. It's great if he sees you as special, but for the long haul, he needs *you* to see *him* as special, and you need to think about this half too.

HIS FIRST GUT REACTION

Your man's **need to be recognized as special** is the first of his four basic needs. His Masculine Pretense requires validation from you. Of course he wants you to see him as all the things that he has striven to become—manly, desirable, and in control. But he senses much more in himself than just this.

If you wish to be different from all the other women he has dated, you will have to go beyond his Masculine Pretense. This image, which he has worked on to send forth into the world, is really very shallow. In his efforts to be "a man," he has submerged his individuality. He needs you to see that individuality and bring it out so that he can see it better in himself. He needs you to see him in a way that he hasn't always dared to see himself.

For you to become *the* woman in his life, you will have to learn who he is apart from the superficial aspects of his life, such as his age, his education, and his income. You will need to appreciate your man for who he really is underneath.

He knows that he has had his share of self-doubts, small gains, disappointments, and victories, just as you have. Like you, he is afraid and embarrassed at times. He worries about what particular people will think of him, just as you do. He is afraid of certain ventures but plunges forward anyhow, just as you do. He has sometimes been outsmarted, he has given more than he got back, and felt foolish, just as you have. His imperfections are part of what make him special. **He longs for a woman who accepts both his strengths and weaknesses—who knows more about him than anyone else does.**

You may be thinking, "How could anyone *not* see him?" He may talk in a louder voice, have a bigger physical presence, and maybe a bigger profile job than you do. In the most superficial sense, you are right; he is perhaps already more visible than you are. But where it counts, he is a victim of his own Masculine Pretense—the pose that society has demanded of him. Because he has been taught for so long to keep his emotional life to himself, it's hard for him to feel truly understood where it matters most.

For men, as for women, it is our emotional life, after all—what we really think and feel, what we worry about and want—that is the most important part of us. Because of his Masculine Pretense, your man has probably had to suppress this most important part of himself, his true individuality. He needs a woman to see him as special, to know what he likes and dislikes, what he wants and what he fears.

All this provides you with a super chance to make a special connection with your man—by seeing him as he really is and by **encouraging him to reveal his true self to you.** If you can be the woman who not only permits him to be real but who also *wants* to know what truly matters to him, you will be freeing him from a form of personal imprisonment. You will get a wonderful gut reaction from him.

As the relationship progresses, if you encourage your man to reveal his full self to you, *you* will become special to him. He will rejoice that he has finally met a woman who seriously wants to understand him.

If you don't do this, it won't matter how attractive you are, or how much you admire him, or how much you do for him. He will develop a negative gut reaction to you. He will feel that you are just another woman making demands of him—that you don't care about who he really is.

To make your man feel special, you obviously have to get him to talk about himself. You need to present yourself as interested, able to listen, and not critical. By doing this, you predispose him to confide in you and ultimately to feel very special himself.

TREAT HIM AS AN EQUAL

Of course, it's wrong to put a man down in the early stages of dating. Less obvious are the dangers of putting a man up too high. Putting him up too high, like putting him down, is a failure to see him as he really is. Many women inadvertently push men away by being too admiring, acting as if the guy can run a company, solve problems, lift automobiles out of the snow, and manage his affairs far better than she can manage hers.

This is insulting to you, and it does a terrible disservice to your man. You can't possibly admire him until you get to know him, and if you start out with excessive admiration, you never will get to know him. You are forcing him to retreat behind his Masculine Pretense, to hide anything about himself that could make him appear weak or disappointing to you. He will simply tighten his masculine straitjacket more—that is, until some woman comes along who really wants to know him.

If you really like this guy and feel lucky that he's in your life, don't put him up too high. Possibly you've been searching for someone like him for a long time, and now he's here. But try not to think of him as the fulfillment of your every dream about the future. The problem with this kind of fantasy is that it's about *you* and not about the man. You will subtly convey to him that you aren't really interested in him, that you care more about the role he can play in your life.

A little unreality is part of romance. But especially before a first date, if you've heard good things about him or met him briefly and think he's great, you run the risk of too much unreality. As soon as you meet him, concentrate on the *actual him* more, and less on what he might mean to your future.

Remind yourself, especially in the first few months, **he is far from a god, he is only a human being.** When you get to know him well, you won't need this frequent self-reminder. As you have your ups and downs together, equality will come naturally. But right now, even if you have to force yourself to think of him as just another person and not the man you've waited a lifetime for, it's worth it. By the way, if you look to him like the woman of his dreams, he is probably trying to overcome his own nervousness.

If he gets the sense that you see him as perfect, he'll want to keep that image going. He won't want to tell you anything about himself that might make him look flawed; yet these are the very things that he needs to talk to you about. By treating him as your equal, you will free him to come out from behind his Masculine Pretense and talk to you about what really matters.

BE NATURAL

Sure, you're a bit nervous. Early in a relationship with a man you like, and especially during the first few months, expectations run high. You have a right to be nervous. Label your tension as *excitement* about him and about the evening, not as fear that you aren't good enough for him. Thinking this way, you are more likely to keep communication lines open.

Your goal right now should be to act as natural as you can—ironically, the way you would act if you didn't really care what he thought about you. **The more relaxed you can make yourself, the more comfortable he will feel about revealing himself to you.** he will see you as able to listen to whatever he decides to bring up. He won't feel pressured to say important things or make himself look good. Of course, this is easier said than done. But you *can* do it.

If it's a first date, a good way to keep the balance is to tell yourself, "This is only one evening in my life. The worst I can do is waste it." You can use this thinking as well later on. Remind yourself that your aim is to have a good time. In fact, go a step further. Help yourself to focus on him by realizing that *he* is on trial with you, too, and not merely *you* with him.

Acting natural, the way you were at lunch with a woman friend yesterday, mostly involves *not* doing things that feel contrived or artificial—and not playing games. You don't have to tell him stories about your rich friends or your brother, the doctor. You don't have to order courses on the menu just because they seem sophisticated. You don't have to keep your voice artificially soft or use your lady-like laugh. Being natural is the ultimate act of trust. The greatest compliment to your man's unconscious is that he is that special guy who puts you completely at ease.

BE POSITIVE ABOUT YOURSELF, AND HE WILL BE POSITIVE ABOUT YOU

If you are a special woman, then he will feel special in your company. When you meet a man you seriously like, it's only human to wonder if you are the woman he wants. Of course you may doubt yourself at moments. But try hard never to say anything bad about yourself.

Your attractiveness can't be measured by individual features. You are more than the sum of your physical parts if you want to be. What makes you more is confidence, a quiet belief in yourself. Not putting yourself up or down. For example, telling narcissistic stories about how great you are would be putting yourself up. Doing this conveys a lack of confidence and usually just makes people feel sorry for you. But also never put yourself down. If you were the most beautiful woman in the world and the brightest, you could still ruin any man's feeling of being special in your presence by attacking yourself.

Don't second-guess yourself. For instance, you've done your best over time to look as good as you can. Maybe in moments of self-doubt, you catch yourself thinking, "I wish I had dressed differently," or "I wish I had worked out more," or "I feel bad that I don't have a better job." Get off that mode of thinking. It is negative and not productive. If you have those thoughts, don't put them into words.

Don't apologize for anything in your life. If he comes to your apartment, don't make excuses for it. "I could have had more space, but I wanted sunlight, and so . . ." Don't explain the worn carpet that you can't afford to replace. If he is highly educated and you didn't go to college, no excuses for not having gone. Either don't discuss it or just say that you didn't go.

Certainly don't say, as a woman patient of mine did, "I know I don't have a great body, but I've just begun a workout program and I'm already losing weight." Avoid apologies in obvious and even in subtle forms. All self-doubt is self-preoccupation. Busy yourself seeing *him* and not taking inventory of your weak points. This is better for you and better for him. If you didn't like this guy, you probably wouldn't apologize, and you would come across better, more natural. If he likes you, none of the things that bother you about yourself will matter to him. And if he doesn't like you, if he is the kind of guy who makes judgements about you based on elements that you can't control (at least not right now), then he's a guaranteed problem, no matter how rich or handsome or polished he may be.

A great advantage to being positive about yourself is that he will see you as a generally noncritical person, capable of being positive about him, even if he is imperfect. This will loosen him up further to talk about himself, and you will both get to the emotional core of the evening. He will want to tell you more about himself and find out more about you.

Speak positively about other people too, about men in general and about the world. Don't fall into the pattern of disparaging people. Maybe you've had one or more failed love affairs, and right now you don't trust men very much. But if you say this—for instance, if you talk as if you think that all men are basically unfaithful, or describe them as all out only for sex, or as irresponsible, you will make this man feel defensive. He is, after all, a man, so how can he be special? On the other hand, if you are positive and ready to see the best in people, he will feel more optimistic about becoming a very special person to you.

THIS IS A ROMANCE—NOT A JOB INTERVIEW

Remember that this a date and not a job interview. You may have been told or somehow gotten the impression that the idea of a first date—or of the first month—is to exchange biographical information. Included would be how old you are, what you do for a living, where you went to school and how far, where you were born, what your future plans are—the standard résumé stuff that you would need to put down if you were looking for a job. The unspoken logic is that people need to know these facts before deciding how they feel about each other.

If things go well, this man will want you to know increasingly more about him. But he doesn't want to tell you everything about him all at once.

For many people, trading résumés is the hardest part of dating someone new. You are probably not 100 percent proud of yours, and if you have been dating a lot, you may be sick of giving your résumé even if you are proud of it. If you are like most women, you have a few stumbling block questions, ones that you hope he doesn't ask. You have worked out your best ways to answer those questions, but even those answers don't full satisfy you.

Maybe you have actually thought, "Wouldn't it be great if I could avoid all this exchanging of data at the start?" If you like this man and he likes you, you will tell him everything about yourself eventually, but not yet. You can anticipate that when he has a real sense of who you are, he will be able to see the facts in perspective.

For instance, you want him to appreciate how young you are in mind and body before telling him your age, that you are five years older than he may have thought. Telling him tonight may bias him against you, so that he'll never appreciate how young you really are. Likewise, you want the chance to talk to him as an equal before you have to tell him that you have a relatively menial job. Why give what amounts to a job résumé—to a man who knows virtually nothing else about you? Facts by themselves can be misleading, and yet it has become too customary to exchange basic facts before two people even know each other. This is one reason why dating is so hard.

He feels the same way. He has his own stumbling block questions, and like you, he has rehearsed how to answer them gracefully, and sometimes elusively. Like you, he would appreciate it if he didn't have to give you the whole rundown at the start. Like you, he wants to make an impression that is more spiritual and romantic than any résumé can convey. **He wants you to see him as he really is and not as he looks on paper.**

Tonight, if this is still a date early in the relationship, he probably wants you to enjoy his Masculine Pretense. He would like you to see him as capable, forceful, and successful, and possibly you do. On the other hand, he probably isn't yet ready to tell you certain facts about himself that he feels may ruin his chances, or at least make him look bad. Of course you have the right to ask him if he's married or currently attached. But maybe he has been married twice and wants you to know him better before he tells you that. Or he works for someone and wishes that he had his own business. Or the car he drove up in belongs to his brother. You might not care about these things, but he does. Like you, he doesn't want to lie, but he also doesn't want to tell you everything as yet. He will remove his Masculine Pretense little by little, as he feels able to.

This shouldn't be a problem for you. You don't need to know

everything about him at once. As anyone who has been in love will tell you, feelings don't depend on résumés. Remarkably, **the best way to initiate a lasting love affair is by *not* asking for vital statistics.** Encourage him to tell you what he really wants you to know by staying away from hard facts. Let him know from the start that you are ready to see who he really is. Don't buy into the accepted wisdom that you have to exchange life data to get a relationship started.

By not searching for this kind of data, you are conveying the message that "I don't need facts to decide how I really feel about you. You are special to me, no matter what your past was." This is a complimentary, and by the way, a very sexy message. It is the best way to get a good gut reaction early in a relationship. If the man turns out to be a billionaire, he will always know that the chemistry was there before you found out. He will always remember that you saw him first as a man and that you liked what you saw.

Remember that a gut reaction is an unconscious feeling that he can't really describe. If you put him on the spot to give his credentials, his mind will wander, and he'll have a picture of going home, taking a shower, and watching a ball game on TV. Obviously, that is not the gut reaction you want. Trust that if you like each other, the data will come out. As we will see next, there are plenty of questions that you can ask to keep things going. These questions will tell your man that he is special to you and that you want to see him as he really is.

THE RIGHT QUESTIONS

The right questions will make him eager to talk. They will invite him to feel, "I hope this goes further." These are questions that show your desire to know the real him.

Asking him for his opinion, or getting him to tell you how he *feels* about almost anything will qualify. With this in mind, your pool of inquiry is limitless. For instance, ask him how he feels about the school that he went to, what his favorite music is, if he likes his job, how he feels about the city he was born in, his childhood, politics, or a movie.

As he talks, he will offer you hundreds of openings for other questions regarding what things *mean* to him, how he *feels* about them. "What gave you the idea of becoming a lawyer?" "Did you like growing up in a big family?" "Do you miss living back in Springfield?" "Do you enjoy traveling so much for your job or is it tough?" Any question that invites him to elaborate on how he feels about what he has just told you qualifies as an attempt to *know the real him*. You will get wonderful gut reactions because you are showing that you want to really know him—not who he is on paper but who he really is and what things mean to him.

By asking questions like these, you are helping him to emerge as an individual. You are giving him a chance that men don't often get in their lives. Remember that he is ordinarily expected to be strong and silent and to avoid talking about trivia. But you are giving him the freedom to do just that.

Not all your questions have to bring him out, of course. Be as trivial as you like. If you feel like it, you can ask him if he has a middle name. You are obviously not trying to gauge how well he will work out as a husband by asking that, except in the sense that if he can laugh with you and have fun about the answer, you will have bonded just a little bit. Remember, the key is to ask either fun questions or those that invite him to reveal himself personally. Avoid questions designed to gauge his status in the world or that would help you evaluate what he could contribute if the two of you began a love affair or actually married.

Let's say that he tells you he decided to be a lawyer after seeing a movie with Paul Newman as a lawyer handling a big case. Contrast these two evaluative questions: "Are you a partner in the firm?" "Do you expect to be a partner soon?" with the following two questions, "What kind of cases do you enjoy most?" And when he says after some thought, "Criminal cases," you ask "Why?" He tells you, perhaps maybe after a moment's thought, "It's a funny thing, I started with a lot of divorce cases, and I think I was good at them. But there's more violence connected with them than in a lot of the criminal cases that come up. I guess people can't get their egos out of divorces . . ." He is sharing with you a deep truth, which he may be in the process of discovering. It may be a very personal and special moment.

Let him take the conversation wherever he wants, and you do the same. Maybe he'll brag, and perhaps with justification. He'll tell you that he got a big bonus and that they like him where he works. As long as he brings it up, go with it. But again, stay away from hard facts. Don't ask him how much the bonus was. Instead, enjoy with him the fact that he is liked and did well. "Who decided on it?" "Did you know it was coming?" Questions like these show that you are interested in the process, interested in him.

With some thought, you can nearly always sense the difference between lighthearted questions that can be fun and those that are covertly fact-finding. Fact-finding questions cause bad gut reactions because the man knows instinctively that you are looking at his data and not at him. For example, if you believe in astrology, you can ask, "What *day* of the year were you born?" but if you ask, "What was your *date of birth?*" you could easily be on a fact-finding mission to judge his eligibility as a husband by determining how old he is. The two questions will elicit very different gut reactions from him. In the first case, he will know that you are really trying to see him and that you are able to listen; in the second, you are trying to see how he stacks up in the age race.

*   *   *

Soon after his divorce, my patient Justin, a very successful market analyst, was eager to meet a woman. Justin had liked married life and was eager to connect quickly with someone for a long-term relationship. I feared too quickly, since Justin wasn't in the best position to make judgments, and he was on the shy side. I was afraid that he'd marry the first woman he had dinner with, but the first two women he dated were so prying with their questions that Justin recovered his judgment fast. He took Ellen, whom he had met through friends, to a very elegant restaurant. She had no appreciation of the food or decor, or of anything about the evening. In fact, she complained that the menu was too hard to read—"Too many foreign words." She asked him if he always ate in "expensive restaurants like this," and when he told her that food and good restaurants were among his passions, she started asking him economic questions that got more and more direct as Justin dodged answering them.

With the next woman, Lisa, Justin volunteered that he greatly missed living with his two sons. Lisa didn't follow up on that emotional issue at all, which was too bad, because Justin was dying to talk to a woman about how much he loved his kids and missed them. When he mentioned that he missed his house, however, which he had built only five years earlier, Lisa followed up eagerly. She asked a few questions obviously designed to assess its worth. When she realized that it was huge, she totally lost control. "Exactly how many square feet is it?" she asked. Justin answered her before pausing to think about the question. "Did you have enough furniture to put in there? Where did you get it?" Justin avoided those questions, feeling very pressed. The clincher to the evening came when Justin suggested that they share some pasta as a second appetizer. "I don't know anything about pasta," Lisa snapped, closing the issue abruptly.

Justin had two extreme experiences of being seen as a *commod-*

ity more than as a *person*. He had chosen good restaurants not to show off his money but to share an experience with Ellen and Lisa that he himself enjoyed. He wanted them to have fun and hoped that he would find someone who would share his interests. What he encountered instead was indifference and rejection of him as an individual.

Of course, you can talk about your own life as well. You too have a need to be recognized, and you may enjoy telling him selectively about your past. But only if he shows interest in you as a person. If he doesn't show interest in you, then he's trouble. Beware of the impulse to corner his attention by selling yourself. If he seems bored with you, cut your losses. It's not your assigned job to fill in every silence and entertain a stone.

Nor should you give in to a man who is obsessed with getting your résumé. You certainly don't have to tell any man more than you are comfortable divulging. During your first few hours together most men will know enough not to ask overtly pushy questions like how old you are or how much money you make. If you are asked an uncomfortable question too early (and even a fourth date can be too early), you have every right not to answer it. "I'd really rather not think about my age right now." Do it lightly, and any man with sensitivity will get off your case.

If a man presses you for too many hard facts before the two of you have truly connected, you have a right to ask him, "Why are these facts so important to you?" Then if he accuses you of not answering his question (a common defense used by prying people), you can tell him that he didn't answer your question either. Let him know that essences and not facts are what matter to you.

Of course, you may want to answer some of his factual questions if you feel they make sense. Maybe he's looking for an apartment in your neighborhood and you feel comfortable saying, "I paid a hun-

dred and sixty thousand dollars for this apartment two years ago." Or
he's told you a lot about himself and you feel comfortable letting him
know, "I've been divorced for three years. We were married for four."

But decide whether answering the question makes you feel
closer to him or more on guard. Being natural, talking about feelings, exchanging attitudes and opinions, with some facts thrown in,
will give your date a verve and a sexuality not possible if there's too
much inventory. Think of tonight as complete in itself, not as a mere
preparation. Convey genuine interest in him as a person, and he will
want you to know more about him.

STAY IN THE HERE AND NOW

The best way to make him feel special, and for you to feel special,
is to convey that this interlude with him completely occupies your
mind. You don't need to think about past, present, or future. This is
the time that counts, and it happens to be time spent together.

Immediacy of this kind makes you as exciting, sexy, and memo-
rable as you can be. Nothing is more intriguing than the moment,
and you will be intriguing if you stay in the moment. Think about
any great experience that you have had, whether it was a movie, a
sports event, a party you went to, a sexual interlude. While it was
happening, you forgot everything that took place before it, and you
weren't thinking about the future either. You were entirely in the
experience, and afterward you remembered the experience as a
high point.

Engross yourself in the present with this special man. Look
around you, and you will have plenty to talk about. **Discuss what
matters to you** in your life right now or in this place, and he will talk
about what matters to him right now. He will feel easy with you and
want to see you again. Nothing is too trivial if it occurs to you. If
you're in a Mexican restaurant and you love the colors and designs,

say so. If it's cold outside, and a funny story suddenly occurs to you about a ski trip you went on, even years ago, tell him. If you're involved in a big project at work and you think it might be interesting, mention it.

Let the topic go where it will. You can talk about nearly anything that you would talk to an old friend about, so long as it isn't too personal or too heavy. Recent events are likely to be in the forefront of your consciousness. This means you can talk about them with a freshness and vigor that will be very appealing. The more open you are, the more open this man will be, so don't censor yourself. Mention nearly anything that you might tell an old friend. Take chances, and he will too. It is when people are willing to take chances that love affairs start.

At a party, Alexandra, a college student, started chatting with a boy about the pros and cons of sororities. She admitted that she was feeling buried in sorority obligations and was starting to wish she hadn't joined. For a second she felt that she had said too much to this stranger.

But then the young man jumped in and said that he didn't really like all the scrutiny he was getting in his fraternity. He hadn't felt free to tell this to anyone else, male or female, to say that he was not a group person. Alexandra's naturalness had liberated him to reveal himself. They had a wonderful half hour, and he ended up inviting her to his formal. He might never have revealed his strong feeling if Alexandra had not been so forthcoming. She had elicited a great gut reaction—the young man could anticipate that time spent with her would be honest, easy, and fun.

Be spontaneous, and this man will know that he is special enough to you to deserve your unguarded self. Don't make the mistake of waiting to learn about what he's really like before you come for-

ward and reveal what you are like. I would say the same to him. If
he's opposed to what you truly believe in and doesn't like who you
really are, you have no future with him anyhow.

Don't withhold so much that you feel artificial and nervous. If
you love opera but fear that he will think it's pretentious of you, the
worst thing you can do is conceal your love of opera. Afterward, you
will run around feeling that your love of opera is a dirty little secret.
If he says that he doesn't like animals, tell him that you love dogs if
you do. You don't want to bring him home and have him be surprised by the presence of your best friend. If he finds you too passionate or effusive, or too involved with what he considers the small
stuff of life—how people feel or relationships—you might as well
know that too.

He will probably be delighted that he can start letting down his
Masculine Pretense with you. He may delight in your love of detail,
the richness of what really goes on in your mind, and in your feelings. He will sense that in getting to know you better, he is giving
himself a chance for the connection that has perhaps been missing
in his life. Cry at the movies if you feel like crying. Laugh at what
you think is funny. You will be pleasantly surprised that even if he
doesn't laugh or cry at the same things, he will be attracted to your
depth.

If you act naturally and aren't on guard, you will find plenty of
subjects that have emotional meaning for both of you: raising kids,
your favorite baseball team, tennis, work, friends that you have in
common, the beggar who just came over to you to ask for fifty cents.
Anything that you have feelings about is likely to be good subject
matter. Allow topics to change rapidly. This can make an evening
fun. As a little girl on a play date with a friend, you knew this
instinctively. But it is every bit as true on this date as it was then.

Silences themselves can be entirely natural. Any man needs occasional breaks in the conversation to digest and process his experi-

ence of the evening and of you. You need them too. If you are tense, you may feel that his not saying anything means that he's having a rotten time with you or that he's pulling back. Or that you yourself look like a loser because you don't have anything to say. Quite the contrary. Silences between two people can be evidence of incredible ease and permissiveness. Don't be an automatic silence breaker. Be as free with silences as you are with conversation and with expression of feeling. Silences are part of the flow.

SHOW HIM THAT YOU CAN IDENTIFY WITH HIM

Being able to identify with him is the ultimate proof that you see him as special. You are demonstrating your ability to appreciate much more about him—the parts of himself he hasn't revealed yet.

Try to communicate to him: "I see you and know what you feel, and I care." To identify with someone—a child, a parent, a member of an oppressed minority group, a pet—is to see the world through that individual's eyes. The first thing that goes when you don't like someone is the ability to identify with him, to enjoy his pleasure and suffer his pain along with him. If you basically can't stand men these days, you'll find it hard to identify with this new guy, and if he has any intuition at all, he will sense it. If you are down on men right now, be especially on guard against negative statements. This man may be the one who will change your mind, so don't ruin things by taking out past grievances on him. If you like him, and men in general, you will know what he's feeling at least some of the time. When he tells you that he was stuck in traffic for two hours, you'll wince. When his promotion comes through, you'll automatically be happy for him.

Even on your first date, and certainly during your first month with him, you can show him your ability to see life through his eyes. You can convey that you resonate emotionally with what he says about himself.

For instance, he tells you about a tough spot he was in—maybe that it pained him recently when a close friend asked him for a big loan. Don't just give him advice. That would be stepping out of any identification. **Simply experience the moment with him.** "Boy, that was a difficult position to be in." Then ask him what he decided and why. You'll have many opportunities to show that you know how he is feeling. You can't connect with a man unless you can identify with him first.

You will identify wordlessly at times, as by simply reaching over and unlocking a car door when he is approaching it from the other side. By that small act, you convey a sense of what he needs. You do the same by thanking him for dinner if he happens to be the one who paid for it. You are not just appreciating the money that he spent; you are saying that you see the thought that he gave to you and to what you might want.

Peter, a young architect, was a patient of mine. He had to come to New York City two years before I saw him and had dated a number of women. But he had broken off one relationship after another, usually early, feeling that he just couldn't connect. One of the reasons that he came to me was to find out what had been going wrong. Then he met Jamie, a woman who had natural empathy and who was a master at identifying with others. Peter hadn't specifically thought of her as having this trait. But his gut reaction to Jamie was profoundly positive. After several dates with her he told me, "I finally met a great woman."

On their second date, Jamie had mentioned that she loved ballet. Never having gone to a ballet, Peter surprised her with tickets. He reported to me that though he enjoyed it only somewhat, he loved her excitement about it. But what moved him most was her thanking him for trying something new, simply because she wanted to go. "She actually thanked me for waiting on line for those tickets," Peter reported. Jamie had said to him, " 'I bet you were there for an hour.' "Actually he had been, and the comment moved him.

Jamie had virtually let Peter know that she had "seen" him standing on that line, just as she might have seen a close woman friend doing the same thing. She had identified with him and made him feel special.

During their early dates, Jamie made it clear that she also identified with Peter in other ways. She sensed that Peter had spent a number of years working too hard—studying architecture and then moving up in his firm. Peter was very touched by her recognizing how alone he was in New York City and introducing him to her close friends. Other women he'd known had recognized none of this, and had left him feeling as alone as before. By much that she did, Jamie communicated: "I see you in detail, and I care about what I see."

Your ability—and willingness—to see your new man as an individual is primary because you can't truly love someone unless you see who that person really is. You can be infatuated with a movie star, but the man in your life wants more—or certainly will want more if your relationship is to last. More men break off relationships because they feel "she doesn't really see me" than for any other reason. Men stay in love, remain loyal despite the bumps in the road that all relationships must endure, when they know that "the woman I love sees me and loves me as no one else ever can or will."

A relationship should be fun, and when you start to see yours this way, you are on the road to getting the best gut reaction from your man. The best way to make a relationship fun is to learn about each other in a natural way, not by exchanging résumés but by discovering each other's true likes and dislikes. Once your man sees that you think of him as special, he will start to drop his Masculine Pretense, and he will feel as free with you as with anyone in his life. Only then will he start seeing you as special too, not as a date but as a lifetime partner.

3

Keeping It Light When You Start to Care

YOUR MAN'S SECOND BASIC NEED —TO TRAVEL LIGHT

Almost from day one, you began picturing what life with your man would be like. You looked forward to change. Being with him would bring positive new experiences—you would decide where to live, you might travel together, maybe you'd start planning for children. You would integrate your family with his.

But the more serious your man gets about committing to you, the more he has another kind of thought. While you're thinking about change, he's worrying about preservation.

You know that your man has problems with commitment, but maybe you haven't thought of it as a neurotic need for preservation. We think of men as being adventurous and of women as the scrapbook keepers, who cherish continuity and predictability. **But men are actually terrified of lifestyle change.** Many women underestimate the depth of this problem. They conclude too fast about their man that he can't commit because he's immature. They see things simplistically. They imagine that their man is afraid of marriage because he'll be forced to give up other women or because he'll be tied down—spending all his money on diapers and station wagons, and never being able to see his guy friends on the weekend.

These concerns may have some relevance to your man. But they are only symptoms. The trouble runs much deeper. With his Masculine Pretense, your man sees his freedom as hard won and as a measure of his virility. He feels that his masculinity depends on his remaining unburdened. For him to give up his current lifestyle completely for a woman may be his ultimate nightmare. He has pictures of more and more changes until there is nothing left of him.

Traveling light, being a real guy who can do what he wants without reporting to anyone, feels essential to his manhood.

He very likely sees women, in this case, *you*—as a threat to his independence. Insulting as it sounds, and *is*, you have to help him appreciate that marriage to you isn't a trap.

Let's say that you've been seeing your man for a while and there's a real chemistry between you. Your man may already be wondering if he is trading "I" for "we" faster than he wants to. Even the few "couple" things that you want him to do may feel frightening—as if they are precursors of a total takeover. It could be as simple as letting you know early in the week if he'd like to go out on Saturday night. Consciously, he knows that this is reasonable. But unconsciously he feels a demand on him that he may picture growing and crushing him. Emasculating him.

Is this irrational of him? Of course. You don't want to be crowded either. You don't want a man who is overly jealous or who asks you to account for every minute of your time or for every dime you spend. But your idea of crowding is much more within the bounds of reason.

You understand that every serious relationship entails giving up some freedom. If you have to drive his kid sister or his mother somewhere, you don't feel like a prisoner of war who might never be set free again. Your time is every bit as important as his, but you probably have more emotional flexibility and willingness to use it in building relationships that matter. To your man, any surrender of his freedom, no matter how brief, can make him feel that he's losing control of his life. Because of his Masculine Pretense, he suffers an exaggerated fear of being imprisoned, a supersensitivity to loss of freedom, as if his whole manhood rested on staying loose and resisting requirements.

Men's need to travel light is excessive and symbolic. Your man's Masculine Pretense, *his need to see himself as a free agent*, ranges from inhibiting to crippling. Men want lasting relationships as much as women do. Nearly every man who looks back on a life spent alone and without constant love is incredibly sad and disappointed in himself. What keeps men single in every case—and this means, in your man's case—isn't lack of love but an exaggerated fear of being confined, which can be his worst tragedy.

Let's look closely at what traveling light really means to your man, at why he holds this illusion so precious that it can make or break a love affair.

TRAVELING LIGHT—MASCULINITY GONE HAYWIRE

To your man, traveling light (in a relationship) implies a life with very few personal demands made on him—of doing almost whatever he wants. He expects some restrictions, of course; he knows that once he's with you, he won't be able to sleep with other women. And obviously he can't run roughshod over you; nor will he want to if he is at all worth your time. But in his fantasy, he still clings to an image that you discarded many years ago—the fantasy of a life in which all is permitted. Few men have completely outgrown the dream of being totally free, of having limitless time for themselves, of owing nothing to anyone.

It doesn't matter that actually living this fantasy wouldn't make him happy, that we all want loved ones to expect things of us. The fantasy of traveling light dies hard in men and never completely disappears. It tends to be much stronger in men than in women because of early training, because of their Masculine Pretense.

In boyhood, while your man was learning all those other troublesome "manly" traits—for instance, not showing emotion and ignoring the "small" stuff of life—he was forming his sense of what a hero is, and of what he wanted to be. A hero, he learned, ventures forth *alone*, without guidance, and reports to no one. Some version of this heroic myth has inspired men from the beginning of time. Only slowly has your man relinquished his vision of himself as a great statesman, athlete, scientist. But he has never fully relinquished his Masculine Pretense, in which he is this kind of hero, a free spirit who need not turn to anyone. To some degree, most men have a horrible fear of being devoured. Even reasonable demands on your man's time may evoke the picture of you as jailor instead of lover.

Underneath, your man wants permanence—a warm, inviting home that will always be there for him. But his identity as a free man, one who travels light, makes him cautious. His conflict over "Should I marry?" is really a conflict over how to reconcile his masculine identity of freedom with love and what love entails. Unresolved problems here are a big reason why men appear claustrophobic—why they are so often accused of commitmentphobia.

Especially early in the relationship, **your man will watch for signs of what life with you will permit:** can he still invite his buddies over to watch the NCAA basketball finals, in which his college is competing? How much time will he be forced to spend with friends of yours who bore him? How much accounting for his time away from you will be required? He interprets the answers as signs of whether his freedom will continue or be snuffed out if he commits himself to you.

Compare his dream of romance with your own. The man you first imagined marrying when you were a girl was handsome, kind, successful, and probably decisive. The greatest of his decisions was his love for you. Even as a child, you perhaps thought of doing things together with this man, maybe of a relationship where you could practically read each other's minds. In your fantasy, closeness and mutual affection were expressed by shared activities—such as having guests to your home or planning a vacation.

You based your fantasy of a relationship on the best of what you witnessed in your childhood. If as a girl, you saw a couple in the supermarket cooperating, you pictured yourself in such a store with the man you would marry. He would be pushing the cart and you would be putting items into it. Or you would be wheeling a baby carriage with him at your side. You even pictured yourself with him during emergencies, possibly staying up together to care for a sick child. If you were lucky, the adults who inspired these fantasies were your own parents.

No matter what kind of parents your man had, however, he almost surely didn't have this kind of fantasy. Even if his parents were perfect role models of cooperation, he visualized that "hero" image—*being on his own*—much more than the image of creating a home. He fantasized about love and sex with a woman, but probably much less about doing other things with her; in his fantasy, she was simply *there* when he needed her. So were the children of his fantasy, they were bright and pretty, but that was it. He didn't picture joint activities, the domestic realities, as you did. His dream was of his being free and of you, the woman, being available and loving.

In the very early stages of your dating, everything is just as your man always pictured it. He *has* his fantasy—of a woman who is available, who is devoted to him, and who requires little sacrifice. As in his fantasy, he doesn't have to change anything about himself or limit himself especially. He's not yet in big trouble for not calling you as often as you want him to. He is not yet sharing a home with you, and there are no children to think about. He is enjoying the combination of traveling light and having you.

In this early stage of dating, however, your experience of the same relationship is quite different. You are hoping for the harmonious relationship of your dreams, but it hasn't arrived as yet. He is still a relative stranger, not the man walking beside you in the supermarket, spotting a favorite item of yours and tossing it into the cart. You are still far from fulfilling your fantasy. For you, this early dating stage is merely a prelude.

It is during this stage, where your fantasies clash, that most relationships struggle or fail. You want change—you want to bring him into your orbit, but he may be happy with the relationship as it is. He would like to have you as lover and friend while preserving his own orbit and the sense that he is in sole control of his life.

DEALING WITH HIS NEED TO TRAVEL LIGHT

Remember that his identity is much more fragile than yours. If a woman friend shows you a picture of a hairstyle that she thinks might look good on you, you either take the suggestion or leave it. There's no harm done either way. You have probably changed aspects of your appearance or of your environment many times. You are *used* to making small adjustments.

But be warned. If you ask your man to change his style of dressing, he's apt to take it as an *attack* on his one identity. Changes of any kind are much more threatening to him than they are to you. Because of his rigid Masculine Pretense, your man may find nearly any personal adjustment difficult. The Masculine Pretense makes men the real hysterics when it comes to adapting in relationships. When faced with the need for even small concessions, many men want to run away and return to a place where they can travel light.

This doesn't mean that all is lost. It only means that as you ease into the relationship, you have to be aware of what we may call euphemistically your man's "special sensitivity."

You've shown that you see him as special. You have recognized his identity, his essence beneath the résumé. By now he should understand that you respect what matters to him—his interests, his habits, his desires—and that you want him to retain as much of them as is reasonable. If he's at all sensitive, he should understand that you aren't there to place burdens on him or to use him unfairly. He should see that you regard him as an independent person and one whom you happen to love.

Still, in every partnership the people involved need to make some adjustments in order to be together, and love is no exception. You can't do all the compromising. Your man has to opt for you, not only in words but by actions in the real world. **No one can travel completely light in a love relationship.**

He has to start realizing that you aren't emasculating him every time you ask him to do something. You aren't asking him to do anything that you yourself wouldn't do.

He has to start trusting you. You are, after all, offering him a lot of new things that he yearns for—a sense of family, of someone waiting for him, the experience of two people traveling in the same direction. With you, he'll be able to loosen his masculine straitjacket and embrace the rush of life that you embody. He should reap a feeling of wealth from all this richness of experience.

But of course it's his choice. If your new life together isn't worth his giving up the few dollars that it will cost him, or the extra time, if he won't make any of the needed "concessions," then this guy may not be worth it.

If he resists even small compromises, then have it out with him early. If he goes on feeling that everything you ask for is too much, he may have a problem that no woman can overcome. Love may simply be less important to him than his portfolio, or his golf game, or whatever he considers his "independence." Cut your losses fast. By staying with such a man, you risk going on in a relationship that gives you little or nothing. Even worse would be the scenario of his giving you what you want, but always grudgingly, and your feeling continuously guilty about it, as if you are defrauding him of things that you don't deserve.

Most men, however, will show enough caring to respond better than this if you are reasonable. As your man gets closer to you, the romance will count more and more to him. Soon he will see that you are offering the emotional richness that he has always wanted. The every-man-for-himself game won't be so much fun anymore.

If you follow some simple rules in dealing with his need to travel light, he'll be only too glad to give you all that you need.

GETTING WHAT YOU WANT WHILE HE TRAVELS LIGHT

You can actually use your man's neurotic need to travel light to your advantage. He'll be so thankful for the space that you give him that he'll *want* to make you happy.

Obviously, you're not going to let your man exist like a loner who promises nothing and drops in only when he's in the mood for sex or sympathy. But you can offer him the sense of traveling light without having to do anything like this.

This is because his need to travel light is mostly an *illusion*, like much of the Masculine Pretense. Because he's so sensitive to offenses against his maleness, very small things that you do may upset him disproportionately. But, on the good side, equally small things can have surprisingly positive effects on him. In a very short time, by even tiny touches on your part, you can show your man that you respect his need to travel light, as no other women he knew ever did.

Just as your man may feel irrationally cornered if you ask him on Tuesday to pin down his weekend, he can feel disproportionately great about you if you offer him some small freedom. "Why should I object if you like to watch *Monday Night Football?* That'll be my night out with my friends."

Like other aspects of the Masculine Pretense, your man's need to travel light has been ritualized over the years. As with every ritual, it is easy to figure out once you know the rules. It isn't full of surprises. There are three criteria by which your man judges nearly everything concerning his freedom. Since childhood, he has associated these areas with manly independence or with being a wimp.

The following three principles will show you how to get what you want while enabling your man to travel light:

1. Keep a fair balance of giving in the relationship
2. Don't be an emotional heavyweight, and
3. Make sure that he has time for himself.

KEEP A FAIR BALANCE IN WHAT YOU GIVE

Of course, you can't literally balance out everything in a romance. that would mean giving each other exactly equal time to talk when you're together, contributing an exactly equal amount of money, dividing chores exactly equally. But even if you could do these things, it wouldn't really matter.

Balance is *psychological* and, especially for your man, is partly illusory. When he thinks of balancing the giving, he is mostly taking a defensive position. He is terrified that he will be asked to change too quickly from "independent" to "caretaker." Unfair and insulting as this sounds, it is not a reflection on you but on what his Masculine Pretense may demand of him.

Two of the most important poses that he assumes as part of his

Masculine Pretense are (1) provider and (2) worldly success. No matter that you have a wonderful career and a staff of ten—he is, in his mind, the hunter, whose job it is to bring home the dinner. This is the source of much that you may like in him: it can make him ambitious, protective, brave, and loving. But though you may enjoy these aspects of his Masculine Pretense, here as elsewhere, it can create problems.

Many of the early problems about keeping a fair balance in a relationship occur around money. Because of his Masculine Pretense, your man may insist on showing you that he is a provider and a worldly success by spending more than he should early in the relationship. Your man may try not to let you spend anything the first few times you see him. This is to impress you and may be an attempt to imply that he makes more money than he actually does. But by acting like a big shot, your man is creating an imbalance that starts to trouble him.

By the time it dawns on him that he can't keep going this way, he may be too embarrassed to tell you that he's over this head. Without giving you any chance to say that you are perfectly willing to kick in your share, he may start to panic and form a picture of you as a grasping woman, who demands more than he can afford. This scenario is unfair but is, unfortunately, quite common.

Women often get lulled into this because they don't understand men's peculiar feelings about money. You probably think about money in terms of the freedom and enjoyment that it can buy. Of course, you want enough for necessities. Beyond that, you'd like some savings to insulate you against emergencies. But you probably also feel that you deserve some luxuries. You feel that money can enhance the joys of life for you and your loved ones.

But even if your man isn't cheap, he will probably have a reaction to money that is very different from yours. Because of the Masculine Pretense, **men see making money as a sign of virility**—it marks them as a provider and worldly success compared with other men. Remember, competition is a strong component of the Masculine Pretense. To him, being broke, living poorly, having to turn to others for money, looking incompetent when dealing with finances—all are desperate forms of humiliation. Beyond thinking about what money can buy, a man is likely to think, "What have I done with my life if I haven't made enough money to gain respect— to be a man?"

For men, money equals potency, and poverty equals impotence to a degree that women find it almost impossible to understand.

When I work with male patients who have inherited a good deal of money, they invariably tell me in early sessions that they made it in some venture, for example, by trading stocks or with some short-lived business. Only after a while do these men feel free enough to admit that they never earned anything but inherited it all. Other therapists report hearing the same lie from their similarly wealthy male patients.

Men's money is their masculinity to a preposterous degree, a fact that you should know, because it will explain a great deal between you. You often hear a woman say, "My boyfriend [or my husband] is going to kill me for buying this [outfit, car, bracelet, gourmet food]. You almost never hear a man say that his wife will kill him for spending too much money or even for losing money in the stock market. The idea of being accountable to a woman, even afraid of her, is intolerable. Women think about the future at least as much as their men do, but seldom with the morbid fear of embarrassment that the man has.

From the start, help your man see that to you money is some-thing used not to offset the cost of a bomb shelter but to enrich a life. Let him see that you care about balancing the relationship just as much as he does, that you are willing to pay what you can to enrich your lives together. Ask to pay your share even in the early stage of the relationship. Discourage him from overspending if you feel he is doing so.

If he has much more money than you do, you obviously can't split all the bills down the middle. But once you start thinking about it, you both know what fair play is. Twenty dollars from you toward a vacation, or concert tickets, or an elegant dinner may equal a hundred dollars from him.

Say you've gone away to a bed-and-breakfast for a weekend with him, and he paid the bill. If it is at all possible, try to pay for a lunch or two. If money is tight with you these days and you simply can't reciprocate in dollars, there's plenty else you can do. Obviously, thank him profusely. (Don't imagine that giving him sex amounts to thanks; sex should be a mutual act, never a form of payoff.) Maybe you can offer to spend time with his niece when she's in town, or go over to his apartment on a Saturday morning and help him refinish his desk.

You can easily show your man that bringing you on board will make him wealthy in all the respects that count. Money is, after all, mostly symbolic to him. In his mind, its an amulet against embarrassment, against the feeling of being unworthy of love. With you, he can exchange a life of working, saving, and fighting against humiliation for the knowledge that he has arrived and that now he has someone to share life with.

The more love he feels, the less anxious he will be about money, and the less he will fear some ultimate disaster. He will want to live now, not later. Of course, he will want to save, as you do, so that he and those he loves will have enough. But money, as the late Quentin Crisp once put it, is the "booby prize of old age." Love is the real prize.

In his desire to show you that he's your true provider and protector, your man may overextend himself in other ways as well. He may volunteer himself as the ultimate problem solver. He can fix

your car, or at least bring it to the "right" person; he can get someone in his office to help you set up your new computer system.
Your man's offers may range from being just what you wanted to
being annoying, unnecessary, and patronizing. Still, your impulse
may be to accept his help either because you need it or because you
want to empower him as a man.

Since you are in a relationship, you certainly have the right to let
your man assume some burdens. But be aware of what you're doing.
Once again, balance is the key. Your man's Masculine Pretense may
compel him to offer much more than he really wants to. And
because he does not register his own feelings, he may take a while to
realize that he is doing more than he intended. When this happens,
he will build up an unconscious resentment of you and will unfairly
perceive you as being too dependent. Not recalling that he virtually
insisted on doing the things he did, he may feel taken advantage of,
and you will pay the price.

Some of the most successful men that I've treated (successful in
the world, though not in romance) told me that women always
want too much of them. As they described their relationships, I suspected that most of the women involved didn't even want the help
but were allowing the man to display his virility and competence. In
some cases, the men ended the relationship because they felt
exploited. In others, it was the woman who ended it, telling the man
that she felt overcontrolled.

Because of your man's Masculine Pretense, there is a thin line
between letting him build his ego by helping you and allowing him
to give too much, after which he will feel bad. Realize this, and
you've won half the battle. As long as you are patrolling the balance,
things won't get out of hand.

Try not to let your man go overboard, even with respect to small
details. If you're meeting for dinner on his side of town, and he
insists on coming through heavy traffic to pick you up, don't let him.

Show him that you perceive pointless chivalry as burdensome to him and unnecessary for you. Turn down six offers that you don't really need, and then it will seem reasonable when you accept help that you can really use. Is much of this symbolic? Yes. But the mind works by symbols.

On the other hand, if you believe that a man should *always* pick a woman up for a date and you require your man to needlessly drive across a crowded city at rush hour to pick you up, he will get a sense that he can't travel light and that your unfairness will only escalate. He will experience your adherence to proper form as a signal that life with you will be the end of life as he knows it.

Being aware of the problem, you can let your instincts guide you. And don't do too much for him either. Traveling light goes both ways. Knowing that loving and being loved are the only real ways to travel light, that they are the wings of existence, can help you overcome all imbalance problems.

DON'T BE AN EMOTIONAL HEAVYWEIGHT

You're used to talking about your emotional life with at least one close woman friend. Good conversations help you stay centered and also help you bond with that friend. You'll probably find yourself wanting to talk the same way with your man as you get closer. But his Masculine Pretense won't permit as much as you might like of this activity. Even if your man has worked on being sensitive, and *is* sensitive, he has less tolerance than you do for discussion of the inner life.

If he seems impatient when you tell him about your mood changes, it's not that he doesn't love you. it's just that from childhood he has been taught to "get on with it" and not dwell on feelings. Athletes, after all, play when they're hurt and don't talk about their injuries. At the core of his psyche, your man feels that he should be this way, and he's most comfortable in an environment where others feel as he does. This gives rise to the form of male bonding found at the gym or on the softball field or even in the bar where his office buddies go after work. Conversation there might sound to you like a series of inarticulate grunts. But that kind of communication feels natural to him, and your probing emotional questions feel unnatural and burdensome.

Over time, as your man comes to love you and trust you, and realizes that you have no desire to emasculate him, he won't feel as challenged by your subject matter. As you enable him to travel light in other areas, he will recognize that it's not your aim to make a sissy out of him. But this will take time.

To help him travel light emotionally (and to help yourself too), limit the time you spend discussing what you *don't* like. Spare him the regular role of telling you that things are better than they seem to you. So your boss didn't get back to you today as she promised, or someone got ahead of you on line at the bank, or the supermarket didn't deliver one of your packages. You can handle it. In "sharing" such trivia with him, you're telling him that the world is a grim place and that you're pretty grim yourself. You're instilling in him the desire to move on to a better world where he can live with a more optimistic woman.

Being light means having a shock absorber built into your own system and not subjecting him to every bump on your road. He has enough bumps on his own. By the way, you have the right to tell *him* to stop complaining about every little thing. When you stop verbalizing the negative, it will retreat in your consciousness, and you will actually feel better and be lighter.

Be careful not to ask for too much reassurance. One of the most burdensome things you can do to your man emotionally is to keep asking him for reassurance. Doing this forces him into an emotional territory that he may not wish to visit at that moment. Admittedly, when you're feeling insecure, you'll have no shortage of questions that you'd like him to answer.

"Do you still love me?"

"Wasn't sex wonderful?"

"We'll *always* be together, won't we?"

You have the right to ask him anything you want, *sometimes.* But not too often. You'll burden him and make yourself feel like a heavyweight. Watch closely and you'll see that his answers won't help you anyhow. You'll feel better for a moment if he says exactly what you want him to. "Of course I love you. More than ever." But ten minutes later, you'll probably feel just as shaky. It will cross your mind that he *had* to say this to get you off his case. How else could he have answered you? If anything, you'll feel *worse* because you will know that you showed neediness and made a demand on him.

If you can resist asking him for reassurance, you will probably feel better yourself ten minutes later. As with negative feelings, personal insecurity often cures itself when you don't underscore it by announcing it. Reassurance questions have a way of evaporating when you don't ask them. Lighten up if you can. Take your chances that your momentary doubts are unfounded and that the relationship is on track. Either it is or it isn't. If it is, you have profited by not asking for reassurance—you'll feel braver and better, and you won't have burdened your man. If the relationship is in trouble, your asking for reassurance won't help.

And don't try to cheat by making statements that are actually thinly disguised questions. For instance, you announce a propos of nothing, "I love you very much." Then you wait for the expected, "I love you too."

Or you say something innocent, like "Karen said that we look like the perfect couple." The proof that this is really a demand for reassurance comes when your man says nothing and you feel worse.

When you ask for reassurance, you come across as less confident and less attractive. Gamble on the relationship by not looking for extra assurances, and your very doing this will make you lighter and more appealing.

Don't inflict coupledom on him too soon. An ultimate emotional terror for your man is the feeling of being steered into a relationship before he's ready. He needs to proceed one stop at a time, and *he* has to choose when to take each step. If you make him feel too quickly that he's part of a couple, with everything planned for him—home, children, college expenses, family obligations—he will see his whole life flashing before him. Even if he loves you and would have trod the route you have in mind for him, he will want to run away.

Your man sees most of the danger signs in the way you treat him in public. Being possessed in private is one thing. But being possessed in public can give him nightmares. Even if he loves you, he may not want the world to see him as signed up for a lifetime. Resist doing anything that might appear as if you are gathering witnesses to prevent him from running away.

For instance, when you're with other people, don't speak *for* him, for example, telling them what he likes and dislikes. ("Oh, Rick never eats arugula. Don't give him that salad.") Avoid "we" sentences. ("Oh, we don't eat beef anymore." Or, "We get massages every Tuesday.") Don't take his hand just to show everyone (including him) that he belongs to you. Take his hand when you *want* to, never to make a point. You will get great gut reactions when he chooses you, but bad ones when he feels restricted by you.

A few years ago, I met two couples at a Christmas party. Lauren, someone I had known slightly, was there with a very handsome man. I actually didn't realize that she was with him during the first few hours. They both circulated freely. When Lauren introduced the man to me, she said simply, "This is Jack—." We got to talking, and Jack seemed like a very nice guy. When I told them that my wife and I would be in Cape May the following week, Jack mentioned that he and Lauren had recently been there together and suggested a wonderful restaurant for us. Only then did I realize that they were a couple.

The other couple seemed stuck together with Krazy Glue. The woman, Chloe, whom I had just met, immediately struck me as insecure with David, the man she was with. She brought him over at once and introduced him. "This is my boyfriend, David. (I had known David for years and had never heard him mention Chloe.) Chloe belabored their coupledom, however. "We just came in from our house in Southampton." (I had been to David's summer house several times. He had owned it long before he met Chloe.)

Chloe used the possessive *"we"* many times. She said that *"we"* are going to Europe next month, and that " *'we'* are redecorating *our* country house." She talked about long-range plans with David, first with me and then with several other people at the party. When one of the women present said that she could never get her husband to take her to the theater, Chloe said that *"we"* go all the time. When desserts came out. Chloe told the hostess that David was on a diet, adding that "we're careful about what we eat, so we'd like to have the nonfat dessert."

When they left, arm in arm, Chloe said, *"We'll* see you again soon. You must visit *us."* Actually, I never did see them again. They broke up shortly afterward. Lauren, however, is now engaged to Jack and will marry him in about six months.

To your man, traveling light signifies that he is still an individual and that you two are freely choosing each other, and not tied together in a knot. No man wants to feel trapped. The best relationships are those that allow a full share of separateness. Trust your man to come to you naturally. Don't steer him too much or he won't come at all.

MAKE SURE THAT HE HAS ENOUGH TIME FOR HIMSELF

In the beginning, your man may want to spend every possible minute with you. But he's probably going to get claustrophobic before long. Time, like money, is a more sensitive issue to men than it is to women. Because of his Masculine Pretense, time, just like money, has a symbolic as well as a real meaning. In his propagandized mind, the difference between a man and a boy is that a man can decide what he wants to do and spend as much time as he wants doing it. It's bad enough that your man's job requires regular attendance; even this feels insulting to his manhood. For him to sacrifice time to a woman—even to you, the woman he loves—can feel emasculating.

Men are constantly kidding each other about being controlled by their wives or girlfriends, and the theme is nearly always about their not having free time.

"Do you think John will be able to come over?"
"No, his wife won't let him out."

"How did you get to come tonight?"
"Oh, my wife's visiting a friend."

Of course, it shouldn't really matter to any man what his friends say. But these other men are echoing a deep fear that many men have—the fear of being controlled by a woman.

Especially if you are headed toward a long-term intimate relationship, you need to understand one other reason why your man needs to step back from you at times. You, as a woman, may find it easy to spend stretches of time alone with him. For you, being close, confiding in someone and feeling deeply, is enriching. Intimacy refreshes you. To some extent, it does the same for your man, but, as we have seen, emotional interchanges also fatigue him quickly.

You will also need your own space and time, and you may have to ask for it or simply take it. Most romances go through a stage when the lovers see each other almost exclusively. After a while, both partners want to spend more time apart and also make up for lost time with friends whom they neglected while the romance was brewing. There's a difference though. During the working-out stage of the romance, your man may need to step back at times more than you do.

After intense interludes together, especially if you have been discussing the relationship, he may need to go his separate way for a while. It's not that anything is wrong. It's simply that he feels momentarily flooded, the way one might feel in a difficult class in school. He needs to absorb what has happened—to clear his head. He may do this by being alone, by watching TV, by exercising, or by playing a sport. Very possibly, he is only trying to clear his machine by engaging in any of these brainless activities, or even by spending time with male friends who stay on the surface level and have a taboo on discussing anything deep.

Your man will judge your lightness around time in two ways. He will observe which of his old activities he can continue. The less he feels a demarcation between "before you" and "after you," the better he'll feel about the relationship. More important, he'll gauge how easy it is for him to escape from you when he needs space. If he can do what he needs to do when he feels on overload, when he suffers his "emotional asthmatic attacks," he will enjoy you more when he's with you. He will return from his time-out loving you more than ever because with you, he could travel light, and you didn't object.

Naturally, even freedom has its limits. If he has to go out for the

evening after any tense five-minute discussion about the relationship, he's doing more than taking a breather. On the other hand, if
he has an urge to tinker at his computer for a while, and you follow
him and keep demanding to know how he feels about something,
it's too much. You each have to decide what's reasonable, and if you
can resist the paranoid reaction that every time he backs off, the
relationship is over, you will help both of you. Even the best
romance has to breathe.

But don't let his need to travel light intimidate you. It's not your
role to serve, to do all the nasty chores alone. Don't completely
abandon your fantasy of togetherness, of his walking beside you in
the supermarket. You have a right to expect him to do things with
you, and you may have to claim that right. Individuals differ in how
much togetherness they require, and you'll have to draw your own
lines. Things will be easiest, of course, if you have strong common
interests, and especially if you enjoy each other's friends. If you
don't, you'll have to work to find things you can do together.

As your romance progresses, when your man sees that you have
no intention of devouring his time or shaming him with his friends,
things will ease up. He'll want to be with you more. He will feel at
home with you and loved, and you will feel secure enough to realize that he's not rejecting you whenever he wants to do things alone.

THE LIMITS OF TRAVELING LIGHT

Although your man has a right to travel light, you have rights in
the relationship too. You have given up certain freedoms to be with
him; you may be seeing less of your women friends, perhaps turning down dates, keeping times open. You don't mind; as a rule, it's
worth it. **But you have a right to ask for certain basics from him,
whether he feels emasculated by them or not.**

Maybe you can live with your man's not calling as often as you'd like just to say "hello," or "I love you," or "I miss you." But there are times when noncommunication just doesn't work, when his traveling light isn't good enough. Just as he wants a balance in the relationship around money, services, and time, you need a balance around emotional communication. After a certain stage of the relationship, he is *not* supposed to let two days go by without calling you. He is not supposed to put you in the position of chasing him. He is supposed to come forward with some emotional communication. You can't be the only one saying "I miss you" or "What are our plans for the weekend?"

You know from experience that if he communicates with you, calling and letting you know his plans and assuring you of his feelings for you, you won't feel nearly as threatened by his being away from you, as you feel when he remains mysterious. You won't mind his doing many things on his own. He has to earn his right to travel light by communicating steadily, and you have the right to ask for this.

Identify your basic requirements. If you are like most women, then high on the list will be his calling you reasonably often and letting you know that he cares. Beyond this, you have special things that matter to you. Your lifetime vision may be to have a man take trips with you, or show some interest in your creative work, or spend caring time with a child of yours from a previous marriage. Identify your requirements and be very clear about them. Make clear your latitude and longitude, and learn his, so that you can respect each other's basic needs.

In the best love relationships, the two people preserve their individuality, as opposed to merging so much that they lose a sense of who they are and who they want to be. Their being together remains a daily choice. Strive for this. Your reward for helping your man travel light where possible is that he will renew his love for you over and over. You will know that you are his choice and that he is yours.

4

Be There for Me. I'm Scared.

To hear women talk, loyalty sounds more important to them than it is to the men in their lives. But loyalty is far more vital to your man than it is to you—*even while he is on the fence about commitment.* You want loyalty because you care about him and don't want to be without him. Even small betrayals hurt because they indicate that he may not want you as much as you thought, and maybe you won't end up together.

He needs your loyalty for this kind of reassurance, but also for a bigger reason. Being betrayed by you (in any of a number of ways) calls his entire manhood into question. **His need for your loyalty is a big part of his Masculine Pretense.** The need to have a woman devoted to him, "my woman," belongs to this pretense. Unfair? Of course. What right does he have to demand your loyalty before he commits himself to you? And what does this loyalty consist of?

Most obviously, he needs the "big, strong man" fiction, just as you need the "beautiful princess" fiction from the man you marry. He needs your sexual loyalty, so that he will feel potent and look potent to the other infantile cavemen around him. He'd like your sexual loyalty in thought as well as in deed, though he's probably afraid to say so. He'd also like you to let the world know that you see him as the answer to your prayers, and never consider him as a compromise. He needs you to loyally see the best in him, especially when things go badly. He needs you to view him as beyond comparison. And he needs you to keep his secrets and help him present his best possible image to the world. You want the same expression of loyalty from him, but he has a special problem.

Your man's Masculine Pretense makes it hard for him *to admit* that he needs your loyalty so badly. It warns him, "Don't show weakness. Don't put power in the hands of a woman." When he finally does fall in love, your man will be watching very carefully to be sure that he is making the right choice. **For him, taking a chance on real closeness is by far the biggest gamble of his life.** Love is, after all, a surrender of power. This is why he is so frightened and depends so heavily on your loyalty before he has a right to it. If you understand his need for loyalty where it expresses itself, you can give him that assurance without sacrificing yourself in the process.

Is all of this surprising, that his being the weaker sex is what makes him so needy of loyalty? It shouldn't be. Think of it this way. He wouldn't be so sensitive if he wasn't so dependent on you. If you can take care of his need for your loyalty in even small ways, you will get amazing gut reactions without any real cost to yourself. His perception of you as loyal or not may well decide whether he wants to marry you.

Even when your man feels hurt by what he considers disloyalty on your part, he may not tell you. But this doesn't make your task impossible. Actually, nearly all men look for loyalty in the same forms. If you know what they are, you can get the good gut reactions that you want without much cost to yourself. Men's loyalty needs fall into three neat categories. Your man needs to be convinced of your:

1. sexual loyalty
2. loyalty to who he truly is, apart from what he brings to the relationship (such as status, money, accomplishments), and
3. loyalty to his presentation in public.

Men's loyalty requirements can sometimes seem excessive and irrational. And often they are. Some men are crazy on the subject of loyalty. Small things can get blown all out of proportion, and suddenly your man is seeing disloyalty where it doesn't exist. But over time you will learn exactly where your man is oversensitive. Ideally, if you take care of the small stuff, big problems will never arise, and as you get to know him better and he comes to trust you, his loyalty requirements will tone down to normal. Of course, in the end you are the one who must decide whether he is asking for more than you can or want to give. No man should ever ask you to be disloyal to people who matter to you or to hand your life over to him. The important thing is to understand exactly what your man's loyalty needs are, and this usually turns out to be pretty easy to do.

As we look at these three forms of loyalty you will see how important they each are.

SEXUAL LOYALTY

Your man will almost certainly want sexual fidelity from you long before he asks for it, if he ever does. He may wait for you to mention the subject, and then agree, as if monogamy is your requirement, not his. But don't be fooled. In most men, the Masculine Pretense is at its height around sex. As soon as your man grows attached to you (and maybe even if he isn't), he will feel desperately threatened by the idea of your having sex with another man.

He may be one of those guys who act cool, who like to make jealousy look like *your* problem, not theirs. But this is the joke of all time. Being the weaker sex, men are far *more* jealous than women are, and they are less forgiving of sexual betrayal. They go more crazy over little things, like your having lunch with an ex-lover, or a man's flirting with you, or your going away for a business conference, than you would if the tables were reversed.

Your man may pretend that he can have sex with other people and not get involved emotionally, while you are so romantic that you can't. The aim of all this nonsense is to hide his desperate need for your absolute sexual loyalty. He may be one of those guys who readily admits that he'd like to have sex with other women, and who makes a big deal out of promising that he won't. But if you said: "I would like to have sex with other men, though of course I won't," he might have an inner breakdown of near hospital proportions.

Most men are incredibly unsure of their sexual desirability, and this gives them a sexual loyalty requirement a hundred times greater than they admit to. Calling men "the weaker sex" is especially true around sex. If the guy likes you, the picture of you in bed with another man, including a boyfriend from the past or your ex-husband, will pierce him emotionally. Sexual competition seems built into the male ego.

Your man may be curious about his rivals. He may ask you matter-of-factly to tell him about past boyfriends, about sex with them. "Who was the aggressor?" "Did you like it?" "How did he compare with me?" "No please, tell me the details. They don't upset me at all. I like hearing about it. It turns me on." Maybe he does get aroused by these stories: at the moment, after all, he is winning a competition, and this can make sex better for a while. But competition is a never-ending challenge. If you had sex with men before him, why not after him? or *during* him? Some men will develop distrust out of such stories. Never underestimate men's jealousy and need for sexual loyalty.

What your man really feels if he cares for you is probably something like this: "I need you to think of me as your only lover. I can't bear the idea that you may have had better ones, even though you say you love me and never loved them. It tortures me to think that you ever wanted another man to make love to you. I'm unsure of myself and I can't bear competition." Your man can see that you enjoy sex and he knows that you probably have a sex history. But you'll do best not discussing details, at least not for a long time. Most men can't take it.

Now that you know this, if you didn't suspect it already, how can you convince your man that if he commits himself to you, he won't have to worry about other men? He will need this feeling for the gut reaction that makes him see you as a wife. Obviously, you're not going to quit your job, or avoid having lunch with men, or never again say that another man is good-looking. And if you enjoy looking sexy, you're not going to change your whole appearance so that he never again has a jealous moment. If you need to talk to an ex-husband about your children, you will.

There are a number of things, however, that you can do to convince your man that you are sexually loyal. And once he has the right gut reaction to you on this front, he won't be shaken by innocent things that you do. As he comes to trust you, he will see you as a wife and lifetime partner.

The first is to **discuss a sexual fidelity pact.** When you want this and feel it's time—it could be the fourth date or the fourth month—don't hesitate to initiate the conversation and say that you want it. Don't worry. If he is at all serious, you won't drive him away. The opposite is true. If he cares for you at all, your insisting on sexual fidelity from him and promising it yourself will make him feel *more* secure with you. The moment when two lovers agree to this in words marks the beginning of a new era—one of deeper commitment than they had. By insisting on his fidelity, you are telling your man that he can expect the same from you. Your request is felt as a promise.

Clarify with your man as early as possible how the two of you will deal with ex-mates and ex-lovers. If he's a stickler about your mentioning every contact with exes, argue it out with him if you don't like his demand. Obviously, if you have children with a former husband, you are going to talk to your kids' dad whether your new man likes it or not. Don't make the mistake of letting your man force you into any agreement that you can't keep. Be loyal to yourself. Make agreements that you can keep without being self-destructive, so you don't have to be dishonest.

If you have to leave another man for this one, do it cleanly. Make clear that sexual betrayal is something that troubles you. You are not so "cool" that you would ever just take it in stride. You are communicating your attitude toward sexual betrayal not just by how you treat this man but also by how you treat others. Even if your new man is complimented by victory over a rival, he will identify with this rival, not now perhaps, but later when he is deciding on whether to commit himself fully to you.

Drew and Ariana, both in their midthirties, were each unhappily married. They met in the office, a big ad agency; they didn't work on the same projects, but they were on the same floor. For a time, they had both been vaguely looking for an escape from their marriages, but they were each too cowardly to face their situations in order to repair them or end them. They kept their marriages going for convenience. Drew and Ariana began their relationship in a

Florida hotel where they were staying during a big agency presentation. A little drinking did away with their guilt, and they ended up in Ariana's room, having sex. Back in New York, they continued clandestine meetings, sometimes in hotels at lunchtime. They each took immense care not to get caught, and they weren't.

Eight months later, Ariana asked her husband for a divorce, and roused by her example, Drew also ended his marriage. But what Ariana didn't realize was that Drew was, all along, having a *very bad gut reaction to her*, in addition to his positive ones. All during their secret relationship, Drew had unconsciously been horrified by his sense of Ariana being disloyal to her husband. Even while he was falling in love with her, he was shocked by her bold-faced lies to her husband. In their hotel room, Drew often listened as Ariana told her husband over her cell phone that she was at lunch with a client. He had heard her make up intricate, very credible stories about why she had to be late on certain nights, or why she had to spend a night out of town.

Ariana had wanted Drew to hear those calls. She imagined that she was showing her devotion to him and a willingness to break all other ties—to throw away the rules, for him. During one of those calls to her husband, Drew stroked Ariana's hair; it was exciting to do this while she spoke to another man. At the time, he had gotten a momentary thrill out of the cloak-and-dagger triumph over his sexual rival. But even as Drew saw Ariana as sexy and desirable, he was accumulating a sense that he could never trust her. His Masculine Pretense prevented him from saying anything about this, however; he didn't want to show vulnerability. He didn't want Ariana to think that he wasn't man enough to handle a little treachery.

After their divorces came though, Drew found pretexts not to tell the world that he and Ariana were a couple. He said that it would be bad for their careers if the agency discovered that they were together. He said that it would make things worse for their divorce settlements; he told her that his lawyer said that they should wait. But Ariana was starting to sense that something was wrong. Within six months of their divorces, Drew broke off the relationship with Ariana, saying that he just wasn't ready for anything serious.

Drew and Ariana came to see me at the very end of their relationship, in a last-ditch effort to mend it. Ariana saw the relationship as having begun on a high romantic note. "We went through hell to be with each other. We were both trapped and the only joy in our lives was being together." Drew agreed, but another feature of the experience was now haunting him. He had loved the great romance and the dangerous sex, but now these memories were dimming. Instead he vividly remembered those phone calls when Ariana, without a tremor in her voice, had lied so easily to the man who still trusted her. Drew had accumulated a disbelief in Ariana's loyalty, which he could not overcome. Those memories were just too vivid, and there were too many of them.

In a later session, in my office alone, Ariana told me about a saying that she had heard, that men never stay with the woman who helped them get out of their bad marriage. "It's incredibly unfair," she said. "I did everything I could think of to show him that I loved him. You don't know how I suffered every night when he went home to somebody else."

She was right, in a sense. But the loyalty issue proved too great an obstacle. She and Drew never got back together. Ariana had underestimated the strength of men's gut reactions to disloyalty, *even when they themselves are not the victims.* When you show disloyalty, even in your man's favor, he will worry that one day, you'll be disloyal to him.

Don't keep other doors open. If you are keeping one or more other men on the line just in case, your new man will *feel* that you are. You run two main risks if you keep these doors open. The first is that you can't be two people, one who has another guy in the wings and another who is demanding complete loyalty from your man. No matter how good an actress you are, he will feel that something is incomplete. The second danger is more obvious. You can't prevent all accidents, and you will pay dearly when he catches on that there are other candidates still around. (A woman I worked with wondered why "the love of her life" dumped her when he found out that she still had a personal ad running after three months with him.)

Some men have the problem of being suspicious. If you're unlucky enough to be with this kind of guy, **never take an accusation of infidelity lightly.** Any suggestion that you're having sex with someone else, or leading a man on, is a serious abuse of you. Assuming that this is your guy and you haven't been seeing anyone else, respond to any such charge as you would to a major abuse. After saying that he's wrong, tell him never to accuse you again or there will be serious trouble. You need to be this tough for your own dignity and also to put his fears to rest. Don't let him form the habit of accusing you or of questioning you suspiciously. Men who do this only make themselves more and more suspicious. Your man will have to learn to trust you and to believe in you in order to feel secure in your loyalty. In any relationship, jealousy fears can arise sometimes, but take care of the small stuff and they won't get out of proportion.

BE LOYAL TO WHO HE TRULY IS

You can be sure of your man's loyalty only if you know that he loves *you*, not the fact that you're pretty or have a good job or have a lot of men interested in you. He needs to know that you feel the same way about *him*.

From the start, you've been showing him that you care about him, that you see his specialness and not just his accomplishments or social status. He needs to know that you would go on loving him even if he lost some aspects that may belong to his Masculine Pretense—his job or his hair, or his big car, or his portfolio. Now you need to go one step beyond recognizing his specialness—**show him that you are loyal to his special essence, which will never change,** even if his circumstances do change a great deal.

You have some very simple ways of doing this:

1. Don't let him see that you chose him by category. Your man has spent a lifetime defining himself as a hero, and no hero wants to feel that he is interchangeable with someone else. Even if it means a lot to you that he's a professional, or tall, or from a good family, focus on *him*, not on his category. No man wants to feel that you chose to be with him just because he satisfies a need of yours—for an escort, a father to your children, an admirer, a provider. If he gets the idea that you want him mainly because he's financially secure or because he's a medical student with a bright future, this isn't the same as your wanting *him*, for better or for worse. How can he feel that you are loyal to him if he senses that you would be glad for *any* doctor, or *any* man who has his own business, or *any* decent man who wants to be married and have children.

You'd be surprised how fast a man can pick up that not just he, but anyone like him, would do. And you would be surprised at how fast his gut reaction tells him to back off and find a woman who would love him, no matter who he was. Every man wants to believe that his woman wouldn't trade him in, even if she could, for someone with more money or a brighter future. Once a man is convinced of this, he can have the kind of gut reaction that leads to marriage. When he doesn't have that feeling, commitmentphobia occurs without any explanation given.

2. Show him that you'd love him even for "better." If you are at all sympathetic, you'll find it easy to pitch in when your man is down. If he's under last-minute pressure, or a parent of his is ill, you can show the kind of loyalty that will give him confidence in you for the future. Being maternal and understanding may be easy when the guy's in pain. But, ironically, it's often much harder for a woman to show a man her loyalty when he's up rather than when he's down.

You are going to discover strengths, opportunities, and gifts that your man has which you weren't aware of, and these will present a special challenge. Maybe you resent the fact that many people listen to your man more than to you just because he *is* a man. You see prejudices in his favor. When he calls the restaurant, you get the table by the window. Not so when you do, and the hostess is much less polite. It may be hard sometimes not to resent him for the sexism in our society. In many places, it's still a man's world, but that's obviously not his fault.

It can be hard to remember this, though, if he gets promotions more easily than you do and now he has the extra cash to add an office to his house or to easily take care of an ailing relative. You wish that you could do these things. Though at times you benefit from his money, at other times it may sting when you realize that he has such advantages. **Be careful not to let envy of him make you less loyal than you could be.** And be careful too never to treat him as if money alone should solve all his problems. You know better.

The more successful a man is, the more sensitive he probably is to this aspect of the loyalty issue. A successful man knows that women want him. But why? It's tricky. He'll want to impress you with his big co-op apartment or with his great job. These are part of his Masculine Pretense. But here's the catch. As the relationship deepens, he will worry that the very things he used to get you interested are all that you care about. Successful men may be paranoid about what you really want. Are you loyal to the lifestyle that he can offer you—or to him?

In my office, I see many successful men who have loyalty concerns about the women they're involved with. The trouble is that these men were already successful by the time they met the woman. They might have felt convinced of the woman's love of them as individuals if they had known her and been chosen by her *before* their success, but this wasn't the case.

Suppose the man you care about and want to marry is already doing pretty well. Let's assume that you really do love him for himself. How can you convince him of your real loyalty to him, that you would have chosen him without the trappings of his present success? How can you make him feel that he is irreplaceable, that even if he lost everything, you would still be with him?

Remember to keep emphasizing the *personal qualities* that made his attainments possible. If he has a successful business, praise him for the perseverance and skill that helped him get it. If he's a professional, appreciate the struggle that he endured to get through school and achieve expertise in a competitive field. If he's a bodybuilder and he wants you to love his biceps, he also wants to know that you would love him if his biceps collapsed. Praise him for his will and discipline. Tell him, if you believe it, that he can do anything that he sets his mind to, and you will be showing loyalty to something about him that he can keep forever.

3. Most importantly, show that you understand that his challenges are the same as anyone else's. No matter how successful or attractive your man is, he will always have ups and downs, just the way you will. His having more money or prestige doesn't make the downs any easier for him to take.

Maybe your man is upset because he feels taken advantage of in a business deal. You can't help thinking that he made more money out of the deal in a few months than you make in a year. Still, because your man's business partner broke his half of the agreement, your man feels cheated, hurt, and unsure of his ability to judge people. Incidents like this give you a very special chance to show that you really care about him. Recognize that even though your man is still financially secure, right now he is suffering, and this is what counts. Give him the sympathy and understanding that he needs, and you will prove that you are loyal to him as a person.

If all you can see is that he is "rich" anyhow and ought to be happy with what he has, you are saying that what counts is what he *has*, not what he *feels*. You would be communicating not just envy but also the belief that people who have money don't deserve sympathy. Acting this way would induce in your man a terrible gut reaction to you. He will feel that you really don't care about him, that you feel that his money can take care of him, and that you don't have to. If you want to share his lifestyle, you must show loyalty, which means never holding money or success against him by being unsympathetic. Many relationships between people with radically different incomes fail because the person with less is envious and lacks sympathy.

The more successful your man is, the harder you may have to struggle inwardly to see him as your equal. But the only way you can have a lasting love affair with him is to see right from the start that he needs the same kind of love and nurturance that you do. If you feel this way, and convey that you do, he will know it unconsciously and have a wonderful gut reaction to you.

A good way to show your man that you see past the externals of his life is to show him that you don't judge *other people* by their social status. Do you treat a waiter or a beggar on the street with respect? Or do you have a different way of relating to everyone, depending on how successful the person is? Your man can't help identifying himself with the underdogs in life, and if you turn your back on people routinely when they slip a bit, he will worry about your loyalty.

*   *   *

Cindy, an attractive businesswoman who had been laboring to meet and marry a wealthy man, finally thought that she'd landed one. She and Luke had been dating heavily for four months. She had been catering to him but was becoming increasingly distraught because he seemed to be slipping away. Luke had once said that he would consider marrying her, but now he had reservations. When he finally told her that this just wasn't for him, she begged him to come to my office once, just to reconsider whether they still had any chance. Luke consented.

It became clear that Luke was an extremely wealthy man, who had taken Cindy on lavish vacations and given her numerous gifts. He had been concerned that she never reciprocated in any way, even though Cindy herself had a very good income. She had persuaded Luke to come with her to see me partly by volunteering to pay for the session and even for the cab that brought them to my office. When they arrived, I asked Luke for his take on their relationship. He said that they could never make a go of it together. "Why?" I asked him. "Well, let me just tell you about coming here," Luke said. "Cindy said that she would pay for the cab. It was eight ninety on the meter, so she gave the guy nine dollars and she talked to him like he wasn't even human."

Cindy couldn't bear to hear any more without interrupting. "What has that got to do with *us?*" she said. "I'm wonderful to you, I do everything you want. I've always been very concerned about your feelings." Luke didn't quite know how to answer her. He tried to explain that he felt bad for the cabdriver. "How could you give a guy a ten-cent tip?" It came out that Luke himself had come from a poor family; he has left college and had struggled to create a huge business, starting with nothing. Now he was employing half his family in that business. It was one thing for him to enjoy flying to resorts with Cindy on his private plane, but quite another to marry her. Cindy protested. "I still don't get it. Why should some cabdriver ruin something beautiful that we have together?" I made an interpretation—or a speculation, whichever you choose to call it. "Because Luke *is* that cabdriver," I told her. Luke nodded, though Cindy still didn't seem to understand. I elaborated, and with Luke's help we clarified what Luke and I both understood intuitively. Luke, like most of us, could identify with that cabdriver, having himself once been in a position of struggle and hope. He was now seeing Cindy not as she acted with *Luke, the rich businessman,* but as she might have acted with *Luke, when he was younger and struggling,* as the cabdriver was, to put a better life together.

Luke had begun to see vividly what he had already sensed, that Cindy wanted the externals of his life more than she wanted *him.* By then he was worried about her loyalty in all respects. Was he really such a great sexual experience for her, or was she faking that, to keep the good life going? And what if things changed, if his business failed or if he got sick or had an accident? Would she still be there, or would Luke get the cabdriver treatment. Pictures of bad scenarios flashed through his mind.

In my office, Cindy acted shocked. She rushed to promise that she would give bigger tips and treat employees better. But none of this was enough for Luke. He had too often seen Cindy act harshly with people who were in her power, and he couldn't avoid feeling very unsafe with her. He was more convinced than ever that Cindy's caring for him was based entirely on *what he had,* and not on *who he was.* He doubted that Cindy could ever truly be loyal to him—to the Luke within, who would always have a little of the cabdriver inside of him.

Cindy could have avoided giving Luke a sense of insecurity if she had followed a few simple rules in dealing with other people. One is that men who are successful still often worry about losing everything. They constantly watch to see if you are the kind of person who would still love them, and they answer this question by watching how you treat people who have less than they do.

LOYALTY TO HIS PRESENTATION IN PUBLIC

The man in your life has spent his adult years cultivating a presentation of himself in public. He almost surely wants people, especially his friends, to see him as attractive, bright, acute at judging other people, and as a good lover. Apart from these near universals, he prides himself on being respected, even admired, for particular traits that you will discover as you get to know him. Maybe a good sense of direction or stock market wisdom are important to him. And if he's a good guy, he wants to be seen as kind and caring, and as a reliable friend. He needs the woman of his dreams to help him project this image of himself—**to be loyal to him in helping him present himself as he wants to be seen.**

You will get a great gut reaction if you prove yourself loyal to your man's social image. He yearns for a woman who will help the world to see him at his best. Conversely, his Masculine Pretense makes him extremely prone to feel humiliated by anything that he perceives as a public challenge.

For instance, David, a patient of mine, was a prolific reader, though he never went to college. He was sensitive about his level of education, but at the same time he was proud of his style of speech, which to me seemed sometimes a bit pedantic. I observed that if another man criticized David's grammar in the office, he felt hurt. When a woman corrected him, he felt much worse. And when Valeria, the woman he was seriously dating, lightheartedly corrected his speech among other people, he felt stung almost to the point of wanting to go home. Granted, David overreacted, but it was obvious to me that Valeria had inadvertently challenged what David considered his right to be a man who could discourse on equal terms with more educated people. You would never say publicly that your man was a poor lover, or that he was inhibited, or that he was having sexual problems lately. You might discuss these problems with a close woman friend alone if they continued, but not in his presence. You realize that your man's *reputation* for sexual adequacy is almost as important to him as sexual prowess itself. Less obvious may be your man's pride in his knowledge of wine or of the best hotels to stay in on business trips or vacations, or his sense of direction, or his driving ability.

Some of the things that your man wants to have a good reputation for may seem incredibly trivial to you. But some men feel almost as reliant on being respected for particular skills or expertise as for their sexual capacity. As you get to know your man better, you will learn which traits of his in particular he wants other people to see and admire.

You have your own special areas where you want other people to see you in a particular way. Your personal attractiveness, your sex appeal, your taste in clothing, or your ability to decorate and run a home may seem to you to be core elements of your desirability. You need your man not just to appreciate your competence but also to help you present yourself as successful in these areas. Loyalty on both sides includes supporting each other's best presentation to others.

Though you can guess some of the obvious qualities that your man prides himself on, you won't be aware of certain others until you know him very well. You won't always know how to enhance him in the special ways that he wants. But you can avoid what he will take as disloyalty.

Never tell any story in public that makes your man look bad. Let *him* tell the story if he wants to, and if he's a loose kind of guy, he well may. But the choice to joke about him must be his. Of course you have the right to disagree with him and to state your opinions about anything. But avoid making negative statements about him in public, even in humor.

If you can legitimately praise your man publicly for a trait that he takes special pride in, you are showing loyalty beyond the call of duty. Suppose your boyfriend, Jon, got you to the party on time through darkness, fog, and sleet, with an unerring sense of direction. If he prides himself on his driving skills, he may appreciate a public compliment for this far more than your last boyfriend would have if that boyfriend took no special pride in his driving.

Is all this need for loyalty in public another indication of the remarkable fragility of men? Yes. But we've already seen that men are the weaker sex, which is why they need loyalty in its numerous forms much more than women do.

Even when arguing, try to avoid making general statements that attack the image of himself that your man wants to present to the world. This can be hard sometimes, especially if you think he's messing up. The key is to combine real loyalty with honest, well-intended criticism.

Brittany, an account executive at a public relations firm, had many friends in the rival firm where Michael, her live-in lover, worked. Michael needed the world to see him as sharply competent and as more talented than anyone else at both doing his job and reading people. But Brittany heard otherwise. Her friends informed her that everybody found Michael impossible to get along with where he worked. More than once, when Michael told Brittany office stories, she would suggest that he wasn't being very fair with someone there. They sometimes ended by shouting at each other. Brittany had no idea what to do next.

Then one day when Michael joined Brittany and her brother and his wife at a restaurant, he reported that he had just been fired. Brittany was angry and about to say that she had expected no less. But she also knew how sensitive Michael was about his ability to deal with people. So instead she simply joined her brother and his wife in commiserating with Michael.

At home that night, Michael pressed Brittany to side with him, saying that it was politics and asking her what she thought could be going on. She resisted telling him how disappointed she was in him. Of course he had been at fault, people had been telling her that this was coming. But she was aware of an even bigger truth. Because Michael was vulnerable just then, he needed loyalty far more than he needed analysis of his job performance.

Michael sensed all along that he had been the cause of his own defeat, and I think that he knew Brittany was aware of this. Probably, he also sensed that Brittany could have said hurtful things but didn't. All that night, Michael experienced a wonderful gut reaction to Brittany, that glorious feeling of love for someone who stays on our side when the world turns against us.

Starting a few days later, she broached the idea that in an office people can be sensitive, even oversensitive. "Maybe you don't take that into account enough." A few months after that, Brittany prevailed on Michael to seek professional help "with office strategies." That was how I met him.

In my office, I conveyed to Michael that although he was probably right on many creative issues, he underestimated his colleagues' susceptibility to injury. People suffer more than they let on when criticized, and they tend to run away. Before long, Michael was doing much better in his new job. He realized how much Brittany had put up with in dealing with him. He was glad to repay her loyalty by examining himself, and soon he started getting the recognition that his talent entitled him to. As he came to a better self-understanding, he also realized how much Brittany meant to him. Michael proposed to Brittany, and she agreed to marry him. Loyalty to your man's public image and to his image of himself needn't force you to sacrifice yourself.

Loyalty issues tend to arise less often as a relationship progresses. As your man comes to trust you, you will hardly have to think about triggering his loyalty fears. Once your man knows that you will support him in front of other people, he will be far more receptive to any constructive criticisms that you need to make in private.

IT GETS EASIER

You won't have to prove your loyalty after six months the way you do at the start of a love affair. You'll enjoy more of the freedom and trust that you deserve. In the beginning, when your man is still frightened of making the great investment of his life, loving you and committing himself to you, he will naturally see shadows of possible disloyalty when you know he really has nothing to worry about. The phone call from your ex-husband, the evening you spend with your two oldest women friends, the conversation with that man at the party, may unnerve him a little. He will want to know at least something of what was said, and you would do well to tell him even if he doesn't ask.

During this early stage, misunderstandings around loyalty can explode into arguments. He may feel shaken when you disagree with him strenuously, even in private, and he may even read disloyalty into your forgetting something small that you promised to do for him. But this won't keep up. As you develop mutual trust, you will spend many more joyous hours and effortless times together, in which loyalty, his or yours, no longer remains a concern.

There's a curious fact here, which you ought to know. Crucial to his getting over disloyalty concerns is not just what you do but what *he* does. If he keeps hedging and not committing himself to you—for instance, if he refuses to say "I love you" or even "I missed you today," if he never talks about long-term plans, if he doesn't introduce you to his friends or try to get to know yours, he will continue to worry about *your* loyalty. Does this sound contradictory? It isn't. We have to take a plunge into commitment in order to trust another person.

He will trust you more after saying "I love you" than he ever could if he doesn't say it. This is why, at your own speed, you need to ask for commitments, even small ones. At a certain stage, you may have to demand the commitments that you need. It's not just that *you* need these commitments, but he needs to make them too if he is ever to feel love and eventually be able to make bigger commitments.

Your man's need for loyalty, like all his four basic needs, springs from deeply emotional sources. It isn't always fair, and you won't always be able to satisfy it. But take comfort in the knowledge that men's loyalty needs are quite predictable. You always knew that men care about sexual loyalty. But your man's need for loyalty in other forms is just as compelling. He wants you to love him unconditionally, and he wants you to help the world see him in the best possible light. His Masculine Pretense is very strong in the loyalty department. In some cases, you won't want to give him everything he wants, and you will have to stay loyal to yourself first. But when you can show loyalty at no cost to yourself, you will get fantastic gut reactions from your man, and he will become less afraid of the idea of committing to you.

5

Give Me the Love That I'm Too Ashamed to Ask For

YOUR MAN'S FOURTH BASIC NEED
—TO BE CLOSE EMOTIONALLY

Your man's fourth basic need is to be close emotionally. An obvious need? On your side, yes. For you, being close to a man is clearly a basic. You have dreamed of a soul mate with whom you can share all your feelings—happiness, anticipation, even sorrow. If you have ever loved a man who withheld intimacy, you know that no form of existence is lonelier, or more depriving. To you, life without love looks sterile. You would have no trouble admitting how disappointed you would feel if you never found a man with whom you could share the intimate moments of your life.

On the surface, your man may seem very different from you in this regard. Because of his Masculine Pretense, he may not appear to need the depth or the continuity of closeness that you do. Men talk as if they don't care about relationships or the special moments of life the way women do. In sitcoms and in jokes, men are often presented as squirming away from some girlfriend, while women are presented as obsessively delving into the meanings of relationships.

As we've seen, emotional exchanges can be so taxing to your man that he may need constant breathers.

But don't be fooled. No matter what your man actually says, in his heart he feels every bit as lonely and desperate for a relationship as you do. It isn't strength that stops him from talking about how much he needs love. It's *weakness*. Because of his Masculine Pretense, your man has fallen into a terrible trap. What he wants most, he also dreads. Of all his basic needs, **your man's need for intimacy is his strongest, but it is also the most embarrassing to him.**

Your challenge is to understand why your man resists his need for intimacy and what you can do to help him overcome his fear. You can help him reach a place where he won't have to reassert his independence by running away from what he secretly wants—love and marriage—just as much as you do.

HOW HIS MASCULINE PRETENSE INHIBITS HIS INTIMACY

The straitjacket that your man has consented to wear—his Masculine Pretense—does its worst havoc in the realm of intimacy. How can he express affection when he considers it a sign of weakness, even emasculating? He was probably only five or less when he started cutting down on expressions of intimacy. He was already practicing to be the hero he still thinks he's supposed to be. In his effort to show the world that he was a man and not a little "mother's boy," he stopped relying on mother and seeking the solace she offered him. Rather, he would go out into the world stoically, and then perhaps come back and protect his mother, rewarding her for her faith in him, but by deeds rather than by showing tenderness or caring.

By adolescence, he was seeing the same stereotypes that you were. He copied the men, who were strong and silent, while the women cried and talked about their emotions. He saw some boys get laughed at for sounding too emotional, and he may well have joined in the laughter, thus separating himself even further from his own emotional life.

He has since been living with a contradiction. His Masculine Pretense doesn't truly run deep. He has never overcome the basic need for affection, which is as strong in him as it is in you. But in his mind, a "real man" shouldn't have been as lonely, or felt as incomplete, as he has over the years. Most men are so embarrassed about their need for intimacy that they won't admit, even to themselves, how much they want it.

Now that you've come along, he may be secretly overjoyed that he finally has a chance for the intimacy that he craves. But his Masculine Pretense stops him from acknowledging this. He certainly can't tell the guys how he feels about you. Men's Masculine Pretense inhibits them from telling even their best friends what they need most and want in a romance.

After your man spends a night with you, and the two of you are incredibly close, he may tell a buddy that the sex was great. But how many men have the courage to say to a friend, even if it's true, "I have needed this closeness for a lifetime. I am lucky to have found her. I feel stronger and better about my whole life." You're up against the Masculine Pretense big-time.

Your man thinks, perhaps correctly, that any emotional talk would make him look bad to "the guys," who are too much in his head. At the backgammon club I belong to, whose members are mostly men, women are constantly calling up their boyfriends or husbands to talk about things they have to do together and firm up the evening's plans. Many of the women ask "Do you love me?"—a question often prompted by the man's distracted tone of voice. The man, whose side of the conversation we can all hear, doesn't want to say "I love you very much" in a warm way because we are listening. So he says, "Of course," keeping the conversation vague. Or if he has to say "Yeah, I love you," he says it with an affected boredom, so that we, unwitting eavesdroppers, will know that he said it under duress.

All of this is very tough on you, of course. Your man is still pretending that he doesn't need the amount of affection that you do, but actually he does. He has trouble expressing his feelings even to you, because letting you know how important you are to him would feel like a confession of weakness.

His Masculine Pretense makes terms of endearment hard for him, even when the two of you are alone. It's not the words themselves that are hard. It's that *saying them* would force him to realize how much he needs intimacy, how lonely he has been, and how much he wants not to be lonely—how much he wants you. He may say a lot during sex, which he can rationalize by pretending to himself that his words are expressions of momentary passion rather than utterances of a lasting truth. Or at other times he can pretend to himself that *you* demand intimate expression. He can give utterance to what he really feels, using the self-deception that he's only saying what you want to hear. He may do nearly anything to conceal his intimacy needs, even from himself. When it comes to accepting our own needs, we men are certainly the weaker sex. His conflict is that you have changed his life, but no one must know—not you, not even himself.

With all this in mind, how can you get him to open up and express the intimacy that he feels for you but is afraid of? There are very particular things you can do to promote intimacy that will help him overcome his fear and free him to seek affection more openly with you.

DETAILS ARE THE STEPPING-STONES TO INTIMACY

Every man wants to be famous to the woman he loves, even if he can't be famous in the world. When someone is famous, the little details of his life matter. His journey counts. Maybe no one will conduct tours to your man's home to say, "Joe lives here." There won't be any newspaper features saying that "the twenty-seventh of August is Joe's birthday." But your man wants the woman of his dreams to feel at least a little bit this way about him.

Since the start, you've been following the details of his life. You have tried to identify with him where you could, and in doing so you've been able to convey strong loyalty. Now as the relationship develops further, you can do more. By the third or fourth month with him, you aren't just learning about him anymore. By now, you know his priorities and have let him see that you know them. For intimacy to grow, you need to show him that you see the big picture of his life—that you have a real sense of where he's headed.

His casual friends can help celebrate the obvious milestones of your man's life. But your special caring for him enables you to occupy the small but very meaningful moments along the way—moments that only someone as intimate with him as you are can understand.

For instance, he's told you that his succeeding with a particular client will lift him to a new level in his business. His doing well with that client matters to him more than he has let on to anyone else. On Friday that client called him at home, and after discussing business, they chatted warmly for a half hour about sports. Your man has been excited all weekend about the implication that he's doing so well with his client that they're becoming friends. It looks as if he's really going forward to that new level of success.

You suffered through your man's doubts with him, and now you can be happy with him over this seemingly small event, a casual phone call. You can feel, with him, the huge implications of his feeling that he is very good at what he does and that he won't have to doubt himself again. You have experienced with him a small but significant moment, which no one else in his life even knew about.

*   *   *

Remembering the highs and lows of your man's ongoing life—the shadings, the details—may come naturally to you. If it doesn't, make a special note to recall the names of the people he tells you about. True, he may want sex with you even if you don't remember anyone's name, including his own. But that kind of intimacy doesn't sustain relationships.

Obviously, you won't remember every single thing he says. But if he has to tell you three times that he's making a big presentation on the fourteenth of this month, by the third time he may feel that you're not really with him. On the other hand, if you call him early on the big morning to say, "I know you're going to do great. You've worked so hard," it will probably mean more to him than he ever lets on. Having this degree of caring has always been his secret wish, just as it has been yours. But his Masculine Pretense hasn't permitted him to ask for it.

If he owns his own business, you may not remember the name of some customer of his who failed to pay him three months ago and greatly disappointed him. But intimacy requires your remembering that there *was* a guy who cheated him and that they had the argument. And to remember some of the details.

Over time, your man will start to notice that you are more involved with what he cares about than any other woman has been. Slowly he will get a sense of being "at home" when he is with you. He will feel more important—more "famous" with you—than with any other woman he has known. If other systems are go, how could he not want more and more of this? To end a love affair with you will mean risking homelessness in a deep emotional sense. Why should he start all over again on a frozen tundra with a woman who may not know or care who he really is?

Of course, as the relationship goes on, you have a right to expect him to be interested in the details of your life as well, and to know your priorities. Because of his training to limit himself to the "big stuff," he probably isn't as sensitive to particulars as you are, but he can learn. Don't let him act as if what you say about yourself or your friends is trivial gossip.

Especially around intimacy, your man may feel a direct threat to his Masculine Pretense. But if the relationship is to continue, he will have to care about you in ways that he wouldn't want the guys to know about.

HE HAS TO EXPRESS INTIMACY IN ORDER TO FEEL IT

You can be intimate and want a loving relationship, but you can't create one alone. More than with any other aspect of your love affair, your man must make his own contribution here. He almost surely cares about you or he wouldn't spend so much time with you. But if you want that caring to reach the level of love that leads to marriage, keep in mind that his caring simply isn't enough by itself. **He has to act on his feelings in order to make them grow.** Only by expressing his caring in words and deeds will he begin to see it as a reality and to accept the depth of how he feels. Goethe, the great German writer, once said, "What we nourish within ourselves grows."

A man may love you in moments, but if he doesn't express intimacy increasingly as the relationship goes on, his caring will diminish. What we *fail* to nourish within ourselves dies. You can lead a man toward intimacy but you can not make him drink. He himself has to take some action. **Your man must make certain commitments to intimacy if he is to reinforce his love, and you must encourage him to do so.**

By inviting these commitments, or demanding them if necessary, you will play a crucial role in deciding whether he turns his caring into a love that lasts.

The first commitment that you need from your man is gigantic, but it won't cost him anything, except perhaps embarrassment. It is a commitment that you can not dispense with. This is the commitment of *words*. Difficult as it may be for him, your man must use terms of endearment—say things that make you feel special. He needs to tell you how he feels about you, and after a while he must say that he loves you. He has to do this for his own sake (as well as for yours), because through the very act of doing it he will realize and *feel* how special you are.

Don't excuse him from saying in words how he feels about you. Women have a hundred tricks of self-delusion when they know in their hearts that their man isn't saying what they want to hear. Don't exempt him, even in your own mind, by saying, "He really loves me but he's too afraid to say so" or "He's just not used to intimacy" or "He's not the expressive type." Admit it. If he is like this, you feel deprived. Don't be an enabler for a man who is emotionally stingy.

Don't let him get away with "Isn't it obvious how I feel?" No it isn't obvious. And if it is, why shouldn't he tell you? If he doesn't, he is keeping himself on the fence, and eventually he'll either leave or, maybe worse, go to the altar reluctantly, as if he'd been led there in chains.

It isn't just that he's depriving you. He is depriving *himself* of the chance to love you more deeply. He has to say that he cares about you in order to care more. His *using* terms of endearment, his expressing love in words, is a necessary gamble on you, on intimacy, and on your future together.

The woman who demands that her lover speak to her lovingly is aware of an important truth. **Your man's telling you how much he cares for you is itself a commitment to you and to love.** It's a stepping-stone to marriage.

Likewise, you need compliments, and **he needs to compliment you.** Obviously, if this man has feelings for you and is attracted to you, he is moved at moments by things he likes—your lips, your eyes, how you look in a particular dress, or how attractive you are generally. Here too his saying so will highlight his feelings for you. If he doesn't say anything when he feels moved by you, he is allowing the moment, the feeling, to disappear quickly. He needs to compliment you in order to intensify his positive feelings, so that he will love you more and make each new level of commitment effortless and natural.

Here again, his Masculine Pretense may get in the way. What appears as shyness in men toward women is really a fear of looking emotional or overwhelmed. It's almost as if your man feels that he will lose his identity, that there will be no turning back if he tells you how attractive you are or how wonderful it is to be with you.

Of course, in reality he can always turn back. But his refusal to compliment you is itself a turning back—or more precisely, a form of never getting started. The guy who never compliments you probably won't marry you. The guy who does is at least accepting his reasons for falling in love with you. Of course, compliments can be insincere (anything can be insincere), but don't use this fact as an excuse not to require them.

In the same vein, he needs to be *generous* toward you to deepen his love. It's one thing to let him travel light, but taking *nothing* from your man is as big a strategic mistake as taking too much. Allowing your man to invest in you wisely helps him to value you. True, if he does too much, he'll resent you. But by now you're aware of the need for balance in the relationship. He has to contribute in order to feel that your love affair is precious. If he never does anything for you, if he takes you utterly for granted, he can't form a serious bond with you.

If your man *wants* to pay for a vacation, or to teach you something that you want to learn, or fix something for you, you've got to let him do at least some of these things. We love people whom we make happy, whose lives we improve. Let him know that he is improving your life by his freely made investments of love and caring and he will want to do more of the same. He will start to think of you as his home base.

ENCOURAGING EMOTIONAL RANGE

As you become increasingly involved with the details of each other's day, you talk together more easily. Your man is probably opening up more about how he feels. For him, this easy emotional flow may be a new luxury. He is having an experience that may feel more natural, more permissive, and more exciting than any he has ever had. It's not just that you are interested in him. It's also that he finds himself feeling free with you.

Your man has probably quit on women in the past because he *was less himself with them* than when he was alone or with his friends. Romance, which he truly cherished, proved too costly emotionally. He couldn't be himself with the few women he cared about because he feared that if he opened up, they would somehow be disappointed. Their interests and expectations confused him.

Your man couldn't be intimate with these women over the long run because he didn't know what they wanted, except that it was more than he could offer. He sensed that he wasn't attentive enough, or didn't understand them enough, or didn't communicate enough. He felt that he was doing his best, but there were always mysteries. These mysteries fascinated him at first but then left him with a sense that the rewards didn't justify the effort, the sacrifice, or the confusion.

He may have had a sense with each woman, as the relationship grew serious, that if he wasn't already a failure, he would be if he didn't try harder. Your man's Masculine Pretense left him feeling that emotional exchanges are menacing and full of danger and criticism. He may still have some of that feeling. This is partly why he still needs time-outs after intense emotional exchanges with you.

If you want him to see you as different from all other women in his life, seize upon this new freedom he has with you, heighten it, and let him feel like *an emotional success*. You can dispel his feelings of having been an emotional failure by making his emotional life with you as easy as it is with his men friends, except that with you he has all the rest. Let him see that there is nothing confusing about your emotional expectations. You want an honest, open exchange, and things don't always have to go your way.

Show him that he doesn't have to watch every word he says to you. Don't brood. Try not to hang on to injury or anger in response to anything that he talks about, even if something has upset you for the moment. If you find yourself so angry or hurt that you can't forgive him for something, try to talk it out with him. Remember that we all overreact to things that happened very recently. Maybe you are doing this. Give your injury some time. Ideally, you will find a way to continue with him.

Don't seize on good moments with him either. Simply enjoy them. Let your man see that you have no desire to wrench huge commitments out of momentary displays of caring. You don't expect him to propose marriage if he says something nice to you, so he can say it with ease. Even during a joyous day together, he can become suddenly serious if he needs to. Give him confidence that if he missteps he can fix things instantly.

This emotional range in love will be exciting to him—and new. he'll need time to believe it because his Masculine Pretense has probably convinced him that he needs to sustain a steady beam emotionally and that he will be held immediately responsible for everything he says. With you, he will discover something, which you have always known, that true emotionality is in constant flux. He will become more intimate with you because he will be more intimate with himself, and accepting of himself, than he ever was. He will allow himself the quick mood changes that his spirit requires. If he can enjoy his own emotional range with you, he won't want to give you up. In time, he will find emotional exchanges less taxing.

Create an atmosphere in which subject matter can change quickly, in which either of you can go from a serious subject to a laugh, to something irrelevant, and then back to the serious subject again. The key is *emotional availability*, the ability to respond to the other person's mood and needs.

You're coming back from a great party, feeling elated, when he gets a phone call that requires his making a big decision fast. Can you join him in his concern, share his intensity, help him make the decision? Or will you refuse to change tones and be angry at him for ruining the evening? Allow yourself to change moods as life changes. Work at being emotionally available. As your man sees that you are emotionally flexible, he will sense that he can travel light with you. On the other hand, if he feels that you can't switch emotional gear, he will fear that marriage to you will be a constant uphill struggle.

Eduardo, a young Dominican living in New York and nearing the end of his surgical residency, had been dating Liz, a New Yorker, for about six months. They had fallen in love fast. Liz was delighted, but for Eduardo the relationship had a complication. His lifelong dream had been to bring modern surgery to the underdeveloped regions of his own country.

Liz liked Eduardo's romantic vision, and her friends were very impressed that he was a surgeon. But Eduardo's refusal to commit to marriage frustrated her. When he hesitated to accept a few lucrative offers to practice surgery in New York, Liz felt disappointed. She urged him, "Why don't you become a rich surgeon here, and get the money to really do some good down there?" Liz was used to men offering her what she wanted. She had been the one to turn down others, feeling that they weren't good enough. But with Eduardo, she feared defeat.

Then the Phone Call came. They were in the middle of a weekend that Liz had planned tightly. They had spent Saturday afternoon with friends, cruising around Manhattan on a tour boat. That night, they had gone to dinner and the theater. Liz stayed at Eduardo's apartment, and they were planning to meet another group of Liz's friends for tennis and brunch on Sunday at eleven. But early Sunday morning, Eduardo's closest friend in New York, Rafael, called to say that he and his wife had had an electrical fire in their home. It had half destroyed their house, and electricians and firefighters were swarming through it to be sure it was safe.

Eduardo took for granted that Liz would rush over to Rafael's with him. He felt astonished when Liz sounded annoyed, even *betrayed*, by his desire to get to the scene. She protested at first. "The fire department is taking care of it. What can we do?" Eduardo told her angrily to go play tennis with their friends. Though she caught herself and went with him, Eduardo could not get Liz's initial reaction out of his mind. His concern about abandoning his own people in the Dominican Republic if he spent his life here with Liz suddenly escalated. He felt keenly that Liz didn't know who he truly was and that she wouldn't come through for him when they faced life's challenging moments. With this concern, Eduardo felt stymied by worries that she would not pitch in when he needed her. Eduardo, who was my patient, asked me to see Liz because he was very troubled not just by this incident but by other unnerving similar misunderstandings between them.

In my office, as Liz spoke, I saw that she couldn't simply be summed up as a selfish person. Rather, she was inflexible. She lacked the capacity for *emotional availability*, which permits a person to alter an outlook so as to stay in harmony with someone else. I learned that Liz had been the only child of an anxious single mother. Her mother had been a successful career woman, not particularly warm by nature, who had dedicated herself to effectiveness at the cost of feelings. As a child, Liz had never experienced emotional availability and had not developed much herself.

She simply couldn't change wavelengths, and I saw that this would deprive her of intimacy all her life unless she developed more flexibility. Eduardo, on the other hand, had grown up in a big house, with many siblings, uncles, aunts, and his grandparents present daily. He would change gears when he went from school to his afternoon job, to playing with friends, to caring for a younger sibling, to helping an elderly relative. For him, the quick interchange of moods, of tones, of loving, of fighting, of laughing and learning were everyday fare. Eduardo realized that he had been feeling vaguely that Liz's rigidity would deprive him of the kind of life he wanted and the only one he knew, one of intimacy and flow.

In my office later, he realized that he might have been willing to settle in New York if he had felt that the woman he was with was flexible enough to accept it if he decided to pursue his dream at some stage later on. Eduardo saw Liz's reaction to the phone call as a microcosm of disasters to come. How would Liz feel if five or ten years from now he asked her to spend part of their year in the Dominican Republic? It seemed to him as if with Liz everything would become an argument—how they would raise their children, whose relatives they would spend time with. Her emotional inflexibility threatened Eduardo, who so valued easy flow in life.

At first Eduardo wanted to break off the relationship there and then. But I helped him see that though Liz had not been as emotionally available as she could be, he was being quite impatient with the woman he loved. The love of our lives seldom comes to us ready made. Perhaps if he discussed the problem more with her, she would become more flexible. It turned out that Liz and Eduardo loved each other enough to solve the problem.

Unless you develop emotional flexibility, you can't possibly sustain love from the man you want. You will always be inhibited by a formal, robotic element in your nature. The interchange of better and worse that love requires may come with unexpected speed. Only two people who have this capacity for emotional availability can truly grow together. It has often struck me that "love, cherish and *evolve together*" ought to be a part of the official promise of marriage, since one of the major causes of failure is the inability of one person to be available to the other and to grow with that mate.

PERSONAL REVELATION AS A PATH TO INTIMACY

As your man tests the waters of intimacy, he is drawing closer to you. He will start revealing to you personal secrets of his that are precious and volatile. Without saying so, or even knowing it consciously, he is starting to invest in you as the woman he intends to be with forever. Love affairs are made or broken in these moments.

From the start, you've been encouraging your man to talk about what matters to him. But even as he has begun confiding in you, his Masculine Pretense has made him unduly cautious. You are used to divulging embarrassing facts about yourself. You and your women friends have light conversations about how you messed up, about things that you're sorry you did or didn't do. But he has been trained to conceal such information. His Masculine Pretense has inhibited him from telling you certain particulars of his life that he thinks might make him seem like less of a man than you think he is.

One thing about any pretense is that you have to sustain it or you look like a fraud. It's hard for him to break down now and tell you facts that he feels might discredit him. As your relationship deepens, he probably *wants* to tell you more, but he wonders, "Do I know her well enough? Will she still accept me? Can she still love me if I tell her particular things?" Once again, he feels he is in the weaker position, and in a sense, because of his pretense, he is.

The trouble is that if, over time, he keeps on concealing facts from you, he will stop himself from welcoming you into his life. How can he see you as *the woman who would accept him no matter what* if he doesn't tell you the "what"? By continuing to play on the defensive, after a certain point your man will be convincing himself that you aren't really a special woman but, like every other woman, you are only too ready to judge him adversely.

You are now ready to take emotional availability up another level. Aim for an atmosphere in which your man can see that you won't be critical of him, almost no matter what he tells you about himself. Remember the value of being positive about people in general. How can he tell you that he was married once briefly when he was eighteen if you criticize all your divorced friends as having made stupid or irresponsible choices? If you say that people in your office have no guts when they don't push for challenging promotions, your man won't be quick to tell you that he turned down a good job because he felt unready for it.

If you have a habit of calling every third person a loser or a coward, obviously your man won't be too willing to tell you facts that could land him in one of these categories. On the other hand, if you seem able to identify with other people and are open-minded, he is more apt to come forward.

When your man does tell you small things about himself that he's not so proud of, consider these revelations as special opportunities to show that you are the right woman for him. Go far out of your way to make clear that these new disclosures don't throw you. Let him know that you see him as the same person he was before he told you whatever bothered him.

Even if you dislike what you heard, you needn't say so immediately. Live with the information for a while. Then, if you still need to talk to him about something he said, bring it up later and as gently as possible. Getting straight on any single fact of his past is less important than keeping the lines of communication open for the future.

Self-disclosure by your man is a huge act of trust that reinforces his feelings of intimacy toward you. Take each revelation as a compliment—a reward that he has given to you for having already demonstrated some degree of caring. Remember that **whenever your man tells you something that he doesn't ordinarily disclose, he is watching very closely to see how you react.** If he likes what he sees, he will draw one step closer to making you the ultimate woman of his life. True emotional closeness comes when you are no longer judging each other's worth by new data.

Once you attain this level of bonding, you will find your relationship almost indestructible. The more he tells you, the more special you become. Among the worst prospects of a breakup is the task of revealing yourself all over again to a new person—not just the basics, but the tiny concerns and secret dreams that you have, the things you worry about. He feels the same way.

I can't tell you how many women have brought a man closer to commitment by defusing a potentially embarrassing revelation.

Derek had backed himself into a corner with the woman he loved—all because of his Masculine Pretense. He and Tara had been living together for six months and were talking about getting married. But Derek had been sustaining a life-lie with her, pretending that he was a college graduate when he had actually quit after two years. He hadn't lied in words, but when Tara had talked about her college roommate, Derek implied that he too had spent a full four years with his college buddies.

The crisis came when the insurance company where Derek worked instituted a policy offering their better employees, including Derek, the chance to get an MBA at the company's expense. At company gatherings, Tara had met a few of Derek's friends who were availing themselves of the opportunity. She encouraged Derek to go for it and couldn't understand why Derek kept hedging and saying that he was too busy.

The more Tara encouraged Derek, offering to make any sacrifices necessary to help him along, the guiltier he felt about lying to her. His deliberately misleading Tara gnawed at Derek and actually stood in the way of his seeing her as a wife. When we lie to people for whatever reason, we want to keep our distance from them.

Finally, because Derek truly did love Tara, he gambled. One night he confided in her. "Actually, I never really did finish college. I couldn't tell you because you worked so hard in school and education means so much to you."

Tara instantly realized that this was a delicate moment, a sensitive one for Derek and a pivotal one for her. She rose to the occasion. "What's the difference?" she said. "It's just a certain number of hours. Look at how brilliant and successful you are at your job. You can finish college easily anytime you want to, if you want to."

They had a long conversation about Derek's future. Tara continued to be supportive, pointing out how fast Derek had achieved respect in his company and how much his friends and colleagues admired him. She convinced him that it would be exciting for her to see him go for more education and, above all, that it didn't matter to her that he didn't have it yet.

Of course Tara felt hurt that Derek had lied to her. But she also realized that he had done it out of love for her and fear of losing her. He admired her too much to let her see what he perceived as his tragic flaw. Tara made the decision not to mention the fact that Derek had misled her but instead to emphasize what they had

together. She realized that intimacy with Derek was more important than any particular fact of their lives.

Derek signed up for college courses, and as he went to classes, he
saw Tara as a real partner in the adventure of his life. He had the
sense that he could tell her anything and expect her to be an ally.
From anyplace on earth, you can go to any other place, and for two
people committed to each other, the going is a great adventure.
They married the following year.

When your man comes to you with a problem, don't feel that you
need to offer him a quick solution. Maybe you have one, maybe
you don't. Far more important than your jumping in with advice is
your giving him time to talk. He needs to know that you will hear
him out. He can go to a professional for a solution—a lawyer, a doctor, a real estate agent. What he needs from you is your continued
love and engagement with him, your understanding and your caring. As he feels your support, he will tell you more, and you will
have nurtured greater intimacy between you. You may or may not
find a solution later.

When he tells you any important fact about himself, think of
yourself as someone playing cards with a friend whose hand is con-
cealed at the start of the game. He is turning one more card faceup,
so that you can see it. If you can, respond to this new card as good
news. He has trusted you to see another "card" of his life. Later you
can decide how you want to play the game.

INTIMACY MEANS SUPPORTING HIS PERSONAL MYTH

All of us are unsung heroes or heroines in our own minds, living a
secret fairy-tale life as well as a surface one. We have a *self beneath
the surface*, what I call a *personal myth*. Our personal myth is the secret way that we see ourselves, our mostly hidden picture of who

we really are, as opposed to the impression that others may have of us in everyday life.

Our personal myth may be taken from parents or other role models, from characters in movies or books. Usually we began hatching it in our minds as children. One reason that women get closer to one another than men do is that they are less ashamed of their personal myths. Women wear their myths about themselves closer to the surface and share them with one another easily.

I've heard many personal myths from women in my office. A successful businesswoman told me, "I love dressing up. I've always seen myself as the prom queen of the family." A woman struggling in college motivated herself by remembering, as she said to me, "From the time I was a little girl, I saw myself as a great architect. When other kids were playing with dollhouses, I was taking them apart and rebuilding them." Another woman, a stay-at-home mother, told me that she always envisioned herself as a great athlete, and she used that fantasy to motivate herself to stay in shape. Women often see themselves as Earth Mother, Love Goddess, Master Psychologist, Superwoman, handling career and family, Beautiful Business Whiz, or Nurturer, like my grandmother.

You may combine several images to make one romantic personality, or you may be different women at different times, as your focus in life changes. Your myth is a magical secret thing that gives value and meaning to your life. You draw on it for strength during the day and it romanticizes your life.

A great tragedy of the Masculine Pretense is that most men feel embarrassed by their personal myth. Far from sharing it as a part of closeness, they hide it. This is one of the silly beliefs about masculinity, that a real man doesn't have fantasies: supposedly he acts and then the world has fantasies about him. But the human being is nothing, life is barren, without romantic images, and the personal myth is our most necessary one.

You can become different to your man from any other woman when he offers you the biggest personal revelation of all—when he lets you in on his personal myth.

As intimacy grows, you will start to learn exactly what his particular personal myth is. For instance, on the surface your man looks quiet, but underneath he is a powerful logical calculator, who can read everyone's motives and never gets fooled. On the surface, your man is a corporate lawyer, but underneath he is an eternally exciting, music-loving, dropout. Your man's myth may include common traits, like honesty or strength. Often men's myths hinge on their knowledge of some particular area, like wine or politics, or the stock market.

Once you start looking for it, it's easy to see what your man's myth is. As he trusts you more, he will start to tell you about his secret dreams, or about the things he feels he might have been. And you can see his myth in action during the day. You will notice, for instance, that your man feels surprisingly hurt if his ability in his special area is challenged. When someone disputes his ability to fix his own computer, or tells him point blank that he's way off on his picture of a certain political candidate, he becomes angry or hurt and clams up. You are surprised at how acute his reaction is until you realize that the attack struck a vital organ of his self-esteem.

On the other hand, when people turn to him at dinner as the computer expert, or ask him what's really going on in Washington, he beams as he holds forth. He has been invited to live his myth as computer genius, or political analyst.

Beneath the surface, many men see themselves as "great lover," "rich provider," "selfless sacrificer," "handsome catch," "could have been a major league player," "risk taker," or "charming guy who screws up a lot."

The greatest intimacy that your man can feel comes when you enjoy him as the special person that he is in his fantasies. **Anyone**

can love us for their own reasons, but we want to spend a lifetime
with someone who also loves us for the exact reasons that we love
ourselves. It's important to support the image that your man pres-
ents to the world. But it is even more important to show your man
that you believe in his dream.

The ultimate bond that leads to marriage is respect for each
other's secret self-image. Your man has yearned over a lifetime for a
woman who will see his personal myth and enjoy it. Interestingly,
once you start thinking about it, you may find that you sensed your
man's personal myth from the start and that you were attracted to
him because of it.

Matthew's friends saw him as a player who was dangerous to
women. He had been married three times and had been seriously
involved with several women in recent years. But in therapy, I saw
a totally different side of Matthew. His view of women, far from
being that of a user, was almost reverent. He fell in love incredibly
fast and was deep into relationships by the time he realized that he
and the woman in his life had little in common and nothing to
share.

In his personal myth, Matthew was very religious and saw his life
as a quest for a soul mate who would be as spiritual and self-
sacrificial as he was. Matthew had always expressed part of his
myth. A successful realtor, he offered considerable time to helping
less privileged people in his church find affordable living quarters.
But it seemed to Matthew that the woman in his personal myth, the
one who understood him and felt as he did, would never appear.

When Matthew came to me, he was feeling depressed and hopeless. The thought of divulging his marital history to a new woman
was daunting. He knew that his record would make him look
chancy and perhaps like a bit of a loser, but he also felt that there
was much more to him than met the eye. I realized that there was

more truth in Matthew's own secret picture of himself than in what the record might show.

In Haley, whom Matthew met soon after he began in therapy with me, he found a woman who was not only kind herself, but was also moved by his kindness. Haley had her own problems on the record; she had been in bankruptcy after a messy divorce and had worked miracles to get herself and her two kids back to solvency. After five years of hard work, she was on a good track. Her own trials had taught her that people's circumstances often don't reflect their true natures. Matthew found it surprisingly easy to reveal his life story to Haley. When he told her that he'd been involved with many women, Haley didn't seem bothered.

Instead of fixating on his failures, Haley was more interested in the charity work that Matthew was doing. She saw his personal myth and loved him for it. She told Matthew how badly she could have used his help when she and her kids were looking for a home. That Matthew was there for women in her position meant far more to her than his marriage and dating misadventures.

Haley's appreciation of Matthew's spiritual side meant everything to him. She saw him as he had always wanted a woman to see him—as he wanted to see himself. Matthew appreciated Haley even more when he discovered that Haley had been warned against him by several friends but had seen the real person through the warnings. Haley's fierce independence and her own personal myth—"I will always do well if I trust my own judgment"—was a chief reason that he fell in love with her.

Matthew and Haley got married, and they have no doubt that it will be forever. **The only romances that truly last are those in which the partners feel loved for the reasons that they love themselves.**

Of all the things that we reveal to the lover in our lives, our personal myth is the most fragile and the most important. Of course, this can't be one-sided. It isn't just your man's personal myth that counts. As in the case of Matthew and Haley, you need your man to appreciate your myth as well. You are not being asked to surrender your life to his fantasy. You need a similar commitment from him, and if he loves you, he shouldn't find it difficult. In fact, he will *want* to love you the way you need to be loved. He will nurture your secret self-image, as you nurture his.

CELEBRATE YOUR INTIMACY TO RENEW IT

Life is organic. Nothing remains unless it is renewed—including intimacy. Once you achieve intimacy, strengthen it by celebrating what you have together and what you have as individuals. As you do so, you will evolve a romantic vision of yourselves together that is even bigger than life.

Over the years, during that period of emotional homelessness, when your man's Masculine Pretense forced him to be a stoical loner, he may have viewed intimate celebrations as "women's stuff." But this is only his embarrassment. Help him see that life with you will be a continuous celebration, the kind he has always wanted but been ashamed to admit that he has wanted.

Because of their Masculine Pretense, men are embarrassed to say how much they want to feel part of a loving family. Few would confess that they want to be treated as kids on their birthdays, or how much they enjoy being taken out to dinner to celebrate their landing a new job, or as a reward for any other milestone. Your man may convey "I don't need these things. They aren't what really count. My life is performance." Or even, "Celebrations are kid stuff." But to the unconscious that's nonsense. In his heart, your man wants to be a fairy-tale hero as much as any kid does. So why shouldn't you have a place in his fairy tale?"

True, there may be bigger celebrations someday. But even if he becomes a giant of industry or a leader of many, and is publicly hon-

ored for his success, your celebrating his graduation, or his first customer, or client, may remain a bigger memory. The quiet, unassum-
ing dinner that you arranged for the two of you, or perhaps with a
few close friends, will mean more because you believed in him
before his success was evident. And if that dreamed-of day never
comes, your celebration now will mean even more.

Don't be fooled by his Masculine Pretense. He wants you to see
through it, and to see him not just as a capable man but also as an
uncertain traveler in the world, as well as a boy trying to succeed.

Because his Masculine Pretense is a straitjacket, your man will
experience great relief each time he loosens it, even a little. Your
seeking intimacy with him, aside from its benefits to you, amounts
to a great rescue operation for him. You are saving him from a self-
inflicted loneliness by giving him an increased capacity to love.

Intimacy is continuous. Your man's attentiveness to you fulfills
his deepest dream. The sense of home that we all yearn for is never
fulfilled by merely being loved. Home always involves the act of
loving too.

PART TWO

Connecting

6

Sex—the Technicolor Experience

Sex, whether it's in bed or on the kitchen floor or in the park, can make your love affair. It can create fantastic experiences that offset bad ones. By lingering in the mind it can bridge people after bad interludes and motivate better understanding. Obviously, sex is not the same as romance, but when it's right, it gives romance its ultimate chance. Once you are lovers, sexual thinking will dominate your fantasies about each other. Its special color will enliven all the time that you spend with your man. It will flavor his fantasies about you when he sees you on the tennis court, or in an airport, or serving drinks at a dinner party. Aftertastes of your body and anticipations of future lovemaking color every impression you make.

During lovemaking, everything is exaggerated, and so are the aftereffects of good or bad sex on your feelings about each other. Good sex can help you and your man over the rough spots that occur in every romance. When your man feels sexually accepted and wanted, a spectacular kind of bonding occurs. He will want to see things your way, and he can easily recover from any sense that you are disappointed with him in other respects.

If sex is good, you are fulfilling all your man's basic needs to a degree that he has only dreamed of. He will feel special, sure of your loyalty, intimate beyond his dreams, and he will experience a lightness in love that he never thought was possible. How could he not want to keep you in his life? He will feel that his long, lonely voyage for love and pleasure with a woman is over.

But your man's Masculine Pretense will also give sex meanings to him beyond pleasure and intimacy. As surprising as this may seem, **nearly all men load sex down with more psychological baggage than women do.** Your man is acutely sensitive in ways that may be hard for you, as a woman, to see.

With the right sexual atmosphere, he will use sex with you to love himself and feel triumphant, and you will reap every benefit. But your man is more vulnerable than you might expect to feeling deprived and inadequate as a lover. Once he feels this way, he will experience a wound so deep that in many cases not even love can cure it.

Don't become so concerned with your own sexual desirability that you underestimate how needy your man is. You may wonder why women who aren't very attractive have rich sexual relationships and get their men to marry them. These woman have hit upon the answer that what makes themselves happiest sexually also makes their man happiest. By fulfilling their own needs, they fulfill their man's needs, and as we shall see, that is the secret to having great sex that leads to commitment.

ATTITUDE COUNTS MORE THAN ACTS

The key to whether sex is great in the way that leads to marriage has much less to do with particular acts than with *attitude*. Look at any newsstand and you'll see women's magazines with lead articles that read like this: "The Two Secrets That Will Improve Your Sex Life" or "What Your Man Really Wants in Bed and Is Afraid to Ask For."

The message is that some new combination of sex acts that you haven't tried will make you stand out in your man's mind so that he'll marry you. Sexual cookbooks have a definite place. Trying new acts and new positions can certainly be rewarding, but do they add to your marriage value beyond improving you as an instrument of pleasure? Or, to put it another way, can merely giving him a great deal more erotic pleasure induce him to marry you?

Maybe in some cases it can. But in most cases, your *attitude toward sex* counts far more than whether you two agree on certain positions or acts, or on role-playing, or whatever. With the right attitude, you'll discover an immense amount about what both of you enjoy as lovers. You can read the articles and books together. With the wrong attitude, however, you can't even talk about sex, and every suggestion you make will feel like a criticism of him. The *chemistry of sex* is what makes it fulfilling or not, what makes it the royal road to marriage with the right man or kills the deal.

Your attitude toward sex has become more important than it ever was because, funny as it sounds, sex is more complicated for men than it used to be—*complicated psychologically.* A hundred years ago when women's sexuality was stifled along with most of women's other rights, men could satisfy their Masculine Pretense merely by seduction. A man could feel manly and look good to his friends if he could get various women to "give in." No one asked the woman how she enjoyed the experience. The sheer fact of conquest was enough.

While men still care about conquest, they have a new burden now. Women want erotic pleasure and know what good sex is. This should be good news for the man who is considering marrying you.

It can make sex much better for him. But now that you are an equal who can "rate" him, your man's Masculine Pretense isn't so easily dealt with. He faces not just the challenge of seducing you but also of following up on his campaign promises with a great sexual performance. For your man, starting to have sex with you can seem almost as much a trial as a source of pleasure.

This may seem strange, since most of us think of men as having sex more easily than women. Men are notorious for sleeping with one woman after another and never calling them again. It's true that men can be more casual about sex with a woman they consider insignificant. (You probably don't consider any man you sleep with insignificant in the same sense.) But once he really cares about a woman, the same guy who seemed so casual, is anything but casual. Most men have a double standard—the woman who doesn't count and the woman who does. After you become the woman who does count, your man is likely to have a hundred early concerns about his own sexual performance.

Maybe you wish he could just go easy, stop torturing himself, and let your love life take its natural course. But he probably can't—at least not without your help.

SEX AND THE MASCULINE PRETENSE

Few women realize how much their man compares himself with other men. You look to sex for pleasure, for intimacy, to be closer. But your man, along with these motives, poor soul, makes love to *prove* that he's a man, as if the verdict isn't really in yet. Depending on how you look at it, his excessive concern is either comic or tragic.

Consider this. Millions of men have married women because they liked the way *they themselves* performed in bed with that woman. A preposterous reason for marriage? Obviously. But that's the point. And men are constantly running away from the scene of what they consider their sexual failures.

If you're very lucky, your man has only a small dose of this illness called Masculine Pretense, but chances are he has more than that. Think about it and you will probably see evidence of it. For instance, he asks you too often if you had an orgasm, or if he was good last night, or he boasts about past conquests. Or he's dismal when he doesn't get an erection.

You may be having a great time in bed and see nothing lacking. But your man's mental process is going incessantly. Even the most relaxed of men is evaluating himself in ways that he can't turn off easily. In your man's mind, he faces the challenge of having to both *prove himself* and *enjoy himself* in a short interlude of time. While having sex with you he has to be aroused early to produce an erection. (And any anxiety can block that.) He needs to know your anatomy, to enjoy arousing you but not too much so that he won't have an orgasm too soon. If he's like most men who care, he will feel that he has to make love until *you* have an orgasm, or else he considers it *his* failure. Ironically, the more he cares for you, the more likely he is to worry, and the *harder* it may be for him to take and enjoy all the pleasure that good sex can offer him too.

It may be hard to convert his self-doubt into self-love if he's so busy attacking himself that he can't perform. But nine times out of ten, if you understand his Masculine Pretense, you can help him to put it aside.

WHY, WHEN, AND HOW?

Very early in the game you will either start off in the right direction sexually, or initiate a chain reaction that may heighten his Masculine Pretense and stop sex from becoming an enlarging experience.

Why, when, and *how* should you have sex with him? These three decisions can be the launching pad for a great sex life. But it's easy to get them wrong, and if you do, they can end a romance before it starts.

Surprisingly, the key is to stay focused on what *you* want and what *you* enjoy. Your being open, loose, and having a good time will make your man happiest if he's even a halfway caring person. But there's a pitfall. The more a man matters to you, the harder it may be for you to do this. Just as your man worries more about his performance because you matter to him, you can expect your own performance anxiety when you meet the man who can be your whole future.

As we answer these three questions, you will see the need to go back to the basics of what *you* want, which isn't always easy.

WHY? CREATING A PRIVATE FANTASY

Your man's Masculine Pretense greatly limits his ability to express his emotions. He can't express deep feeling in nearly as many contexts as you can, and this makes sex a vital realm to him emotionally. During sex, while pretending that he is reacting merely to physical arousal, he can be his real self. He can fulfill his desire for intimacy and reveal his needs.

This can make sex a paradise of expression for him, perhaps even a more exceptional one than it is for you. For your man to have this magical fulfillment, he needs to feel that you want sex with him for purely emotional reasons and because you want to be there.

To create the right atmosphere—a sex life that both of you will want to continue forever—try to make sex a dream world and keep it that way. Give sex a place of its own. You should both be able to look forward to it as a refuge where fantasy and reality meet. Sex is your own world for keeping secrets and for trespassing boundaries by mutual agreement. It is love's conspiracy, where you and your man are royalty, and ordinary rules and pressures don't apply. Sex is a realm where you can both be spontaneous with no deals made.

This means that you should **trust the sexual experience to speak for itself.** Never use it as a deliberate device for any purpose. Sex is not for indebting your man, even for getting him to say that he loves you during the act. You may want to hear this desperately, but now isn't the time to talk about changes that you think he needs to make. Nor is this the time to exact a promise: "This is so beautiful, why aren't we together always?" A remark like this is terrible for a man to hear when in the throes of passion.

You know what it's like when you're in a wonderful clothing store. You're looking excitedly at dozens of gorgeous clothes and accessories, trying to take them all in. You're ready to buy some, maybe to spend a month's salary, when suddenly a salesperson comes over and starts pushing you to make a purchase. "Which do you like?" "Let me show you what just came in, it's perfect for you." "You look like a six." "Do you want to try that on?" Suddenly, you don't want to buy anything. All at once your pleasure is gone. You feel pressured and you want to run out of the store.

That's what it's like for your man when, in the middle of sex with him, you start asking him to commit himself, to see you in the future, to marry you, or to do almost anything. Your man will be acutely oversensitive about your tying in sexual pleasure with making even the smallest request or demand.

You are in each other's arms after lovemaking. You are each still savoring the height that you reached and reexperiencing each other's flesh, each other's love. It flashes into your mind that you need him to do something over the weekend. Without thinking, you ask him, "Would you mind driving me over to my mother's on Saturday to pick up that carpet?"

Suddenly the tune goes false. The whole experience changes. You can see it in his expression and feel it in the room. Your man feels demoted, as if you had punctured the lovemaking—as if you said that the entire purpose and meaning of it was false. Does this sound extreme? It certainly is. But so is his Masculine Pretense. His manhood rests to a large extent on his belief that you want him for himself with no strings attached.

Your man has a sixth sense that will tell him why you are having sex with him. In a shorter time than you might imagine, he'll spot wrong motives and feel hurt by them. Your man has probably been with women who went to bed with him because they were afraid of losing him or because they wanted things from him. He didn't feel special with them or truly intimate, and he wasn't fully convinced of their loyalty. They were in a sense lying to him, they weren't loyal to his personal myth of himself as a lover; he came to feel that they were exploiting this very myth. He felt taken. Unconsciously he sensed that he could never travel light with them and that everything—including sex—would have to be paid for.

Just as you want a man who will sweep you off your feet, who will fall in love with you and share everything with you, he has the fantasy of a woman who wants *him*, and *wants sex with him* for who he is. The less encumbered your motives are for having sex with him, the better; he wants you to see his very essence as compelling. Even the most fantastic sex from a purely physical standpoint won't overcome a feeling that you want him for reasons other than for himself alone. Attitude is all.

Sex is a realm apart. Within its confines, all is permitted, so long as neither of you is using force or doing anything against your will. In this magical realm, no sex act is kinky if you both enjoy it. Or if you want to think of it as kinky to enjoy it more, that's up to you. Breaking the rules is part of the game. Sex is a place for art and for fantasy; whether you play roles in words together or only in your mind; whether you talk during the act or choose not to; whether it's in the dark or under bright lights; how often; what the acts should be; whether you repeat positions or keep varying them—no one can tell you what's right for you as a couple. No one has any rule book. The very fact that sex can be so good makes it feel as if you are breaking the rules, getting more out of the experience together than is permitted. **The only perversions in sex are its use for purposes other than for pleasure and intimacy.**

WHEN? EARLY. EARLY. EARLIER THAN YOU MAY THINK

Okay, you want to have sex with him for the right reasons. When do you start? Forget about *him* for the moment. Think about yourself. You're bound to have some concerns. Even if you really like the guy, sex is a gamble. What if you get involved with him and he never calls you again? If you can't handle this (and there's no stigma in not being able to), then obviously you're better off waiting until you know the guy much better.

Or possibly some trait of his disturbs you. For instance, you feel that he is overly critical. Maybe he tends to disparage people for being impulsive or too emotional, or you heard him call a woman "oversexed." Maybe you sense that he's picky and judgmental. Last night he sent the butternut squash soup back with "profound disappointment" because "it wasn't quite hot enough." You wonder how he'll judge you, and you nervously anticipate his thinking that your thighs are too big or your breasts are too small. Here too you can wait. You may be glad you did.

Of course, as we've seen, if your motives for sex are demanding or misguided, then nothing can put a man off faster. Don't make him your lover in a hurry just so that he won't get away. He'll sense that he is being used and that you have a secret agenda. Or maybe you're both stoned or drunk, and suspect that you got that way because things aren't really right between you. Again, wait.

Drunken sex can make both of you feel disgusted with yourselves and each other even if the relationship would have had a chance. If the two of you are right together, you will have other opportunities. But, assuming that everything is right and natural, **sex is put on earth to satisfy all your man's basic needs as well as your own.** This runs counter to a lot of advice that's given, especially by parents and older people, who are more aware of mistakes they made than of opportunities for love that they lost. Because this man is so special to you, you yourself may buy into warnings to wait a long time, which can do you more harm than good.

If this man wasn't so special to you, you might go home with him tonight. But because you think of him in terms of your future, you may see things too much through his eyes and not enough through your own. **Thinking too much about his picture of you can ruin your sexual timing and create distance instead of intimacy.**

Look out for thoughts like "Maybe I shouldn't so *soon*" or "Maybe he'll think *less* of me" or "Maybe I'll lower my *value*." With these motives, you would make sex more a strategy than a spontaneous act of desire.

Bring spontaneity back. The best way to break down your man's Masculine Pretense and set the right chemistry for lasting sex is to show him that you can be swept away by him.

Will he think of you as too loose if you have sex with him, say the fifth time you're with him or well before that?

In my experience, women who imagine they lost a man because they made sex too available are either mistaken or were lucky to lose the guy. Any man who thinks of you as "easy" because you went to bed with him sooner than he thinks you should have is dangerous. He may see sex as dirty and the woman's role in life as holding the fort for purity. If so, he has a lousy view of women. If he requires innocence, he'll stop loving you once you aren't a complete innocent anymore. If he needs you to be afraid of sex, he's a very insecure character, and you ought to be wary of him. He'll have plenty of other unrealistic standards for you to live up to. Let him find someone else willing to spend a lifetime fitting into his mold. You deserve a man who enjoys you as you are.

Far more women have lost out because they allowed a potentially great love affair to fizzle into a limp friendship. With a basically decent guy, it's best to maximize the early excitement in the relationship by igniting the kind of sex life that will start him thinking of marriage.

Your man will always remember that you were as eager to make love as he was. He'll enjoy the memory of those early times, the sense that he is attractive to you, even compelling. Those early days of how the romance started will stay in his mind and replenish love later on. He will likewise remember if you subjected him to a murderous courtship with sex as a reward. Later, even more than now, he will feel that all the desire was *his*. After this scenario, you can tell him he's sexy every day, but if that were true, why did he have to qualify in so many other ways first? Prolonged courtship without sex is insulting to the male ego; it's a form of rejection.

And what about the common belief that men want virgins? Is this really your man's secret fantasy? Almost certainly not. The fantasy woman that nearly all men talk about in my office is sexually experienced. Don't forget that competition with other men is a big part of the Masculine Pretense. Underneath, he feels that the ultimate proof of his masculinity would be success with a woman who has had the best lovers. Men dream about sex with supermodels whose affairs they read about. I've never had a male patient whose fantasy was making love to a virgin. The virgin is a default choice opted for by men who don't want to be judged and found lacking. An experienced woman's passion, her compliments, her *desire* mean a lot more to a man.

In fact, it's actually dangerous to act like a virgin, awed by everything he does. For one thing, you are putting pressure on him to be more of a sexual leader than maybe he thinks he can be, and giving him a lot to live up to. You are playing right into his performance anxiety. Besides, when he does prove himself to the virginal you, he will still be unconvinced of his true masculinity. He'll go on dreaming of a woman who knows her way around sex, who isn't afraid, and who is willing to choose her lover early.

If he sees you as an experienced woman who is appealing and who has been with other men, everything you offer will be much bigger and more attractive to him. Lasting intimacy can be only between two lovers who have choice and who choose each other readily.

And what about the advice that he'll want you more if you play hard to get? You've seen women who never have sex early in a relationship. Their policy is: "Make him work for it and it will matter more." Some of these women get men to fall all over them by acting bored, unmoved, and disappointed. As you watch an attractive guy lavish attention on one of these narcissistic creatures, you wonder why he's putting so much effort in for so little. One minute you may feel like warning him to quit. The next, you envy the woman for her strange hold on men. If your own love life is going badly, maybe you have the thought, "Guys don't treat me like that. I wish I could be like her. I'd give a lot less and get more, and I'd be happier in the long run."

Narcissistic women who play at being distant and unreachable often do get men to run after them. Certain kinds of men rise to the challenge. They mistakenly imagine that coldness is a sign of sophistication and worldliness. They blame themselves for not making the grade with the woman, so they keep trying.

But hard-to-get as a tactic works only in the short run. You can sometimes stimulate pursuit by making a man feel inadequate—by denying him sex or even acceptance. Even a successful man, if he's attracted to you, may break his neck to please you initially. But he's pursuing you because underneath he feels unworthy and incomplete. You have induced in him these feelings of inadequacy, which he is trying to overcome by proving his worth to you. Deep down, he knows that he is making a fool of himself, that he is giving much more than he is getting.

As time goes by, he'll resent you for having made him miserable. He won't stay without sex forever, of course. But after a while he will desire you *less*, and by the time you "give in" and sleep with him, the romance may be almost over. He'll have sex with you then because he has earned it, but he'll feel anything but special. He will soon start getting even with you for what he feels was massive mistreatment of him. When you want something from him, he will withhold it, just as you held yourself back when you had power over him.

In my office, I have often watched men who felt tortured by a woman's remoteness over months or years. As time went by, I could see that the woman herself had ceased to matter. The chase became everything, the man's desire to feel whole by getting the woman to sleep with him and say she loved him. When the man finally got what he wanted, he made sure *not* to give the woman what *she* wanted—not commitment of any kind and certainly not marriage.

Early sex, if you have it for the right reasons, can get you both over many difficulties later on. Your spontaneity distinguishes you from women who have tried to use sex as a way of making their man feel obligated. When you express your desire early, without putting your man through unnecessary paces to prove himself, you are making a positive statement. But, of course, this never means that you should gamble on unsafe sex. You can't take chances when it comes to safety, and no man who cares for you in the slightest would want you to. Do whatever you feel you need to do to be sure that sex with him is safe.

HOW? ESCAPING THE BERMUDA TRIANGLE

Remember the advice about your early dating. Be spontaneous and natural, and express your feelings. This is every bit as important, though perhaps a little more difficult, when you begin sleeping with your man.

Don't let love inhibit sex. The more a man matters to you, the harder it may be to have uninhibited sex with him. You want to be on your best behavior, and this may put you on guard too much. **But if you bring spontaneous sex into the most respectable love affair, it will make the love affair better.**

Some women see themselves as unfortunate because the marriageable men in their lives all seem to be boring lovers. Often *they* are the ones who get boring as soon as marriage enters the picture.

Lori came to me because her program to marry a successful man wasn't going as planned. She was tall, willowy, and very attractive. She was a successful lawyer working in the contract department of a sports agency, and I imagined that she was capable and attentive to detail. Lori stated simply what had brought her to me. She wanted to marry a man who was rich and sophisticated. A few in this refined category had loved her, but sex with each of them had been lousy. Keith, her most recent, was very wealthy, good-looking, and had wonderful style. At first when he talked about marriage, Lori had been thrilled. They had traveled together to luxurious locales, but a lush bed in an ornate room offers no assurance of good sex, as they both discovered. After their last trip to Europe, Keith had accused Lori of using him as a consolation prize for her broke, college lover, whom Lori had often talked about. Lori hadn't denied this convincingly. Finally, feeling confused and deeply hurt, Keith had ended the relationship.

Lori seemed hesitant to tell me a complicating factor, but after a while she did. A few months earlier, Lori had gone to Bermuda alone, to snorkel, sail, and think over her relationship with Keith. On her third day there she had met Willem, an officer from a Dutch cruise ship, in the hotel bar. Knowing that she would never see him again, she seduced him. The sex was fantastic, uninhibited, and frenzied for three days. Though Keith never found out, he may have sensed that his stock declined even further when she returned.

Describing her affair with Willem, Lori said, "I wanted to feel like a woman again, and I did." After calling Willem "a good lover and very uninhibited," she said, "I knew from the start he was only temporary. The guys who I could marry are never the ones I have times like that with."

I asked her what she meant, and she told me about Chris, the other man she had almost married. Five years earlier, she had met Chris at her first law firm. He was from a very wealthy Chicago family and had showered her with attention. After a yearlong engagement, Lori had backed out. Like Keith, Chris had "bored" Lori sexually.

We continued to work together for a few months when one day Lori came to my office flushed with excitement. She had met a man she was very attracted to, at a party given by her agency for one of their athletes. She had gone over to him. "John is great looking, in amazing shape, I think he's a trainer with a fitness camp somewhere." They had talked a lot and danced together. She had told John, "I usually hate suspenders, but you look very sexy in them."

They'd had a few drinks and both confessed that they'd had "some great times" with people they met on the same Caribbean island. "I would have gone home with John last night," Lori said. "But he had to leave early with some guys he was with. We exchanged numbers. If he doesn't call me, I'll call him."

Almost immediately, John called her, and Lori was eager to see him. But when Lori came in after the date, she looked confused. It turned out that John was rich and influential; he owned a chain of stores in the Midwest and had just bought a minor league baseball team.

They'd had a quiet dinner. Upon finding out who John was, Lori had suddenly become restrained. She told me, "Now I'm sorry I said so much about my past." There followed a self-critical flurry, which I had never seen Lori indulge in before. "Maybe I should have worn a suit. I don't know what got into me, wearing leather pants, I thought he was just some trainer who was attracted to me at a party." I asked Lori, "Did John saying anything about what you wore?" "Yeah, he said I looked great, but he would say that anyhow."

I could see that the evening had been a strain for Lori instead of a joy. From the moment she'd found out who John was, she had begun taking him too seriously. There had been no more touching, no sexual innuendo. Lori no longer thought about going home with him, as she had the first time she saw him.

Though John was still new in her life, Lori had already entered the perpetual triangle, having to decide between husband and lover. Even when there wasn't a lover in the picture, *he existed in Lori's mind*. When she was with a marriageable man, she was haunted by the image of an exciting lover somewhere out there. Men in both categories sensed this of course; they could sense that Lori was waiting for some adventure that didn't include them. Naturally, they could hardly feel special around Lori, and unconsciously they doubted her loyalty.

Lori and John went out for a month or so, and when John pressed for sex, Lori finally went to bed with him. But she was passive and nervous. The experience was flat for her, and for him. The relationship with John was ending fast.

I felt an urgency to help Lori in case she could save the flagging relationship with John. I asked Lori to tell me more about her days with Willem to help us understand what was so special about him. Why was her Bermuda affair so much better than this one?

Lori told me that on her first day alone with Willem, she had been as aggressive as he was. They'd had intercourse on the beach and had masturbated each other in the ocean. "I would never do anything like that with John." Knowing that she'd had only three days with Willem, she phoned him the next morning, saying that she was horny. There was plenty of sex and sex talk, and while making love, she told him exactly what she wanted. "I knew I'd never see him again, so I thought, 'Why not?' "

With Willem she hadn't talked about the past or the future. Sex with John was full of overtones about what it might imply about their prospects as a couple. Sex with Willem was the essence of traveling light. It was the exact opposite with John.

Lori was so depressed that she was ready to give up and break off the relationship with him. Psychoanalysts would look at Lori and say that she has a classic problem—the "split imago"; the men she likes remind her of her father; they are successful and well behaved, so she has "incestuous" feelings toward them, which ruin sex and make the relationship antiseptic. She can let herself go only with the outsider, the man who gives the impression of wildness and impermanence. The curse of Lori's psyche, they would say, renders her incapable of having sexual feelings for a man she respects.

But this theory makes it seem as if a woman like Lori can't change a self-destructive pattern. Women who have trouble enjoying sex with the "right" guy aren't eternally cursed. Of course, not every man will be right for you, but if you are attracted to a man to begin with, there is plenty that you can do to keep that attraction going and build on it.

I had to help Lori see that the key is to act as naturally with the man who counts as with a man who you see as only temporary. **The**

best way to insure that you'll have good sex tomorrow is to have sex as if there *is* no tomorrow.

Over the next few weeks, I showed Lori how she herself was creating the pattern that messed up her sex life. I got her to see how naturally she had acted with Willem and the other men who "didn't count." With Willem, she had been aggressive, said she was horny; she had been honest and done what she wanted in bed. During sex with Willem, she was passionate, expressive, and kinky when in the mood. **She had felt desire and shown desire.** She had turned him on and turned herself on.

Lori had been embarking on that same loose, sexy path with John before she saw him as a "marriage candidate." I reminded Lori of how attracted she had been to John the first moment she saw him. She'd thought of him as very attractive and was preparing for an affair with all the same anticipation that she'd had about Willem. Then when she learned that John was *more*, he became *less*. Once John became potentially important to her future, Lori quickly forgot how attractive he'd seemed, and by suppressing a whole part of herself, her erotic side, she entered a very different kind of relationship. By behaving in this whole new way—passively, formally and anxiously—she was turning John off and turning herself off. **She was letting thoughts of the future destroy the present.**

Months earlier, Lori had made Willem feel special, attractive, and chosen. Now she was denying John all these same feelings by concealing her erotic desire from him. As the total pursuer by the time they had sex, John couldn't feel special or light, or intimate. I explained to Lori that, if anything, her reluctance was telling him that he wasn't a romantic lover but just someone Lori was afraid to displease.

"Is it over?" she asked me.

Of course I couldn't say for sure, but I could ask her an important question. "Can you go back to that first evening when you saw John as a sexy and good-looking guy?"

Lori answered immediately, "I sometimes still see him that way."

"That's where it has to go," I told her. "Whatever happened after that took you off the main road. See if you can move ahead with John sexually as if you had no future with him beyond that of being lovers."

Lori was able to return to her initial approach. A few nights later, when Lori had an impulse to make love, she forced herself to come right out and say so to John, just as she would have to Willem. When she did, she felt anxious, almost as if she were propositioning her boss. But John was delighted. They passed up the show that they had tickets for and went back to his apartment.

This time Lori's sexual behavior toward John was utterly different. She allowed herself the freedom that she would have taken if John were just a one-night stand in Bermuda. During sex, she expressed her every desire, allowing herself to make noise and being aggressive at times. When she failed to have an orgasm during intercourse, she put his hand on her clitoris and showed him how to masturbate her. She began really enjoying sex with John for the first time, acting in bed as if it didn't really matter what he thought of her. They remained on the right road. John was for the first time enjoying all the benefits of lovemaking with Lori, and their intimacy grew rapidly.

Showing sexual desire is the ultimate compliment to a man who cares about you. If he's a decent guy, this doesn't mark you as a fallen woman, only as a woman who has fallen for him. As the woman he loves, who also wants him sexually and who doesn't hide her desires from him, you make your man feel special and offer him an intimacy that he has only dared to dream about.

You can help your man shed his Masculine Pretense during sex by being who you really are. The answer to the question of *how* you should have sex is any way you want to, as long as it's what you truly want.

LET'S FACE IT. YOU'RE PROBABLY AT LEAST AS EXPERIENCED AS HE IS

Give your man the full benefit of your experience and openness to sex. In an important respect, you are probably *more* experienced than your man is even if he's had sex with many more partners.

It occurred to me that before I was twenty-one, I had taken a number of girls out, but mostly to the same three or four places—to dances at my social club, to my favorite bar, to a certain flashy restaurant where they greeted me in French and I could show off my language skills. The girls I dated were either impressed or unimpressed by my faltering French, or by the way I danced, or by me. Because my experience and confidence were limited, I made my evenings very much the same, as most young men (and older men) do.

These same girls had of course dated different guys. But even if they had dated considerably less than I had, they'd usually had a much broader *variety of experience.* One of the guys a girl dated might be a football freak who introduced her to his fellow jocks and took her to a game at West Point; another was broke and brought her to a diner where he and his friends hung out. Another had rich parents and brought her to fine restaurants. Another, perhaps a much older man, took her on a weekend to the Caribbean. Nearly all of these girls had been to many diverse events; they had seen far more than I had; they had gone to operas and ballets and been exposed to a wider range of customs and environments.

This holds generally. Because men plan out most dates, women have a much more various experience in dating. Women, being the ones invited, as a rule enter the different games that men contrive for them. And nearly all men tend to repeat their game, staying, as I did, within their own comfort range.

It's the same when it comes to sex for those of us who are more adult. The average guy has his own pattern of how he makes his sexual advance, for when sex happens, where it happens, for the things he says, and for what he does in bed. He does virtually the same things with all the women he sleeps with. This means that a woman who has slept with four guys has probably had far more variety of experience than a man who has slept with a dozen women. She has sampled four different programs, had four lovers who differed widely in attitude and approach. In contrast, the man, as the "leader," has mostly repeated a single experience over and over.

Even if you've had less sex in terms of number of lovers, your range of actual experience may be much greater than your man's. This isn't a negative, it's what secretly turns men on over the long run, once they get past their Masculine Pretense. It relates to what your man may think of as your *mystique*. He may well see you as having deep secrets, a mysterious appeal, and he's not wrong. Give your man the benefit of this experience—your spontaneity, your passion, and even your knowledge.

Even beyond experience, you are probably stronger than your man is sexually. You know this, and he senses it too. A woman can usually have sex longer, have more orgasms, get started more predictably, and not have the same impotence problems that her man has. A woman can even fake sex better. (But don't.) Keep all this in mind if you are worried that he is judging your body or your attitude, or anything in your approach.

Men have always tried to console themselves for performance or arousal problems by blaming the woman. Male patients of mine who are having sexual troubles will often say to me about their woman, "She gained weight." Or "She's getting older." They would rather say that the woman isn't good enough, crediting themselves with fine discrimination and taste, than admit that they just don't get aroused as easily as they used to.

When a man in my office starts talking about the pros and cons of some woman's body and mentions certain aesthetic blemishes (as if he has none), I often remind him that when he was nineteen, those "blemishes" wouldn't have bothered him. He would have been desperate for a woman half as attractive. "Let's face it," I tell him. "Maybe it takes more to arouse you than it used to."

Never accept an attack on you—your physical features or your technique. Starving yourself or going to the gym five days a week won't made any difference if the man you're with has arousal problems or is inhibited. *Attitude* is everything, and the critical preparation is to pass a rule for neither of you to blame or apologize for anything you do in bed. This is an ultimate maxim for traveling light and for loyalty in sex. The art is to keep sex unencumbered for both of you.

7

When Worlds Collide—His Friends and Yours

Your friends are your personal treasure, handpicked, tested, and proven over many years. Since you *chose* them, they are even more indicative of your values and beliefs than your family members are. Different facets of you shine in them. They represent aspects of your personality and your interests. You have turned to your friends for strength and confided in them over time, and though you've likely had your share of conflicts with them, you need your close friends and feel a debt to them. Your life has been an adventure concurrent with theirs, and you want it to continue that way—*with the addition of your man.*

As you weave your man into your life, your fantasy is that he and your friends will hit it off at once. They will love him and be delighted with your choice. In this fantasy, your man will enjoy them and look forward to being with you in their company.

You may also picture your man raising your status with certain women friends. You know that a few are secretly competitive with you, and it would be an added kick if they envied you for being with this guy.

In all, you think of your man as part of your harmonious social picture. If he never wanted to spend time with your close friends, you would have plenty of embarrassing explaining to do. You might eventually have to choose between him and them.

Your man thinks of you much less this way. Sure, he wants his friends to like you and perhaps envy him for "his" woman. But how you get along with his friends means much less. In fact, if he could spend time alone with you and then rush off to be with his buddies without you, this might be ideal. Unlike your friends, who want to include him, his friends won't feel hurt if you're not with him. Quite the contrary. Even if they like you, he might get extra credit for his ability to leave you home. Having an attractive woman who lets him travel light, one who is loyal to the point of letting him do whatever he wants: what a lover he must be to have achieved this! This may sound cynical, but in many cases it isn't much of an exaggeration.

Your big problem with *your* friends is integrating them with your man. And your big problem with *his* friends is overcoming their reluctance to lose him to a woman—any woman.

Fortunately, however, though the input from friends on both sides of a romance is real, it won't be decisive unless you allow it to be. Never forget that **you and your man have the final word over whether this romance will succeed.** At times, when things go wrong, you may feel tempted to blame his friends. But his friends don't have the power to make him end this relationship. And yours don't have that power over you either. If either of you wants to end it, it will be your choice, not theirs.

Remember too that during the relationship, if he joins his friends in making destructive choices, they are *his* choices, and no one else's. He's making them because at some level he *wants* to, whether or not another person is inciting him. And the same is true for you.

The good news is that if you two talk and evaluate what's going on when friends complicate things, no outsider can ever ruin this romance. In fact, if you really talk honestly, no outsider can even cause serious trouble between you.

INTRODUCING YOUR MAN TO YOUR FRIENDS

As you and your man come together, you are merging two mythical worlds. Your friends are a major part of your personal myth, but they don't belong to your man's myth. They aren't automatically the valuable additions to his life that you may imagine them to be. To him, they represent *change*, and, as we've seen, because of his Masculine Pretense, your man is very resistant to change. You can't just throw him together with your friends as effortlessly as you would bring a new woman friend into your social group.

As your man enters the foreign territory of your social life, all his basic needs will spring up. He'll wonder if he can become more special to you than your lifetime friends. Can he compete for your loyalty? He will have his usual conflicts about expressing intimacy toward you in front of other people. And he still wants to travel light. He hopes that your friends will see him as a desirable partner for you, but at the same time he fears losing independence and being shoved into coupledom too soon.

Very likely, your man will start meeting your friends long before you meet his. Some of your woman friends, especially any who have been involved with the project of your romance, will clamor to meet your "mystery man" ASAP. But be careful. Socializing, like sex, has to be done for the right reasons. Just as your man can sense if you're using sex as a bargaining chip, he will sense it if you are using your friends to judge him or to make points with him. He will instantly doubt your loyalty.

Men in my office have often said something like: "She took me to a party last night to have her friends look me over." The man feels manipulated and reduced in value. How struck by him can you be if you need other people's opinions? Men also sense it immediately when you shove them into the company of rich or successful acquaintances (people who may not be real friends) simply to make yourself look good. Your man may be impressed, but he will know that he's being set up. Make sure that when you bring your man together with your friends, it's because you think they'll enjoy each other's company and have a good time. Any other motive is a manipulation.

It should go without saying that it's a bad idea to introduce him to women friends who are competitive with you or prone to say negative things about you. But, of course, you won't always know ahead of time. A woman patient of mine reported being stunned when someone she thought was a friend said to her new man, "I hope Emily stays with you longer than she stayed with the last two." The guy felt shaken, and my patient had to give him plenty of reassurance after that.

If you find yourself extremely nervous about introducing your man to *any* attractive women, then maybe you have good reason. Either it's too early in the relationship to bring in wild cards, or you suspect that he isn't ready for a monogamous relationship with you. Ask yourself, "What am I worried about? What scenario do I fear?" Do you see him as too weak to resist a possible flirtation by one of your women friends? Or worse yet, do you imagine that whenever he is in a room with attractive women, he'll go after one? Whether you see him as a vulnerable victim or a predator, the fact is that you are feeling very insecure with him right now. Ask yourself why. Maybe your man has been giving you subtle reasons to doubt him.

Perhaps he's very critical of you or talks about other women in a way that suggests that his mind is still open to new relationships. If so, a heart-to-heart talk is needed. You have a right to know where you stand. Your man doesn't deserve to meet your friends until you feel that he can be trusted with them.

On the other hand, you may be prone to feeling insecure about any man who matters to you. If so, then it's best for you to fight this fear by trusting your relationship with your man and his caring for you. He chose you from a whole world of women. Proceed on the belief that he will continue to do so.

TAKE IT EASY—HE'S MORE AFRAID OF YOUR FRIENDS THAN IT SEEMS

When you start introducing your man to friends, keep in mind that because of his Masculine Pretense, he will worry that he is no longer number one with you. Expect loyalty issues to surface early. In fact, even before he meets your very close women friends, your man may have a vague sense of unrest about them on several scores.

For one thing, he surmises that your friends knew all about your great love affairs and followed them as they unfolded. They were with you when you obsessed about another man, they knew that you had great sex with him, and they suffered along with you when that dream flickered and died. Your man may fear that his relationship with you is still trivial alongside some great love affair of your past.

He may also suspect that your friends are following your relationship with him in intimate detail, judging his manliness as you report it to them. His Masculine Pretense rebels at this. It troubles him that these strangers are in a position to judge him. He wants their good opinion, but he fears them, and he resents the power that they wield over you and him, even if they treat him well.

It may sound as if you're facing a dilemma as hard to solve as it is to win the lottery—getting sixteen straight digits right. But a single key provides all the answers.

Once you've decided who will meet your man and when, stop thinking. Don't micromanage him. **Having brought him together with your friends, keep your hands off.** Just let the chips fall where they may.

This means **no prepping your man on how he should behave or dress.** Don't sell your friends to him or propagandize. Let him form his own judgments about new people without trying to steer him in advance.

As your social lives converge, don't issue him rules regarding how often he has to see your friends, how he has to behave in their company, or how he has to feel about them. He'll decide which ones he likes and which ones he doesn't. Allow him to discover your friends and make them his own in a casual way. If you pressure him during this initial stage, he'll end up disliking people whom he might have liked a great deal on his own. He'll see you as being controlling and your friends as obligations.

Obviously, when you bring your man into your social life, you can't expect him to hit it off with every one of your friends. Your hoping for this is like the vision in the painting of the peaceable kingdom where all the animals live together harmoniously.

If your man gets into sparring matches with certain of your friends from time to time, don't worry about it. He certainly has disagreements with his own friends. Maybe it's fun for him to debate about politics. He's robust, and so are your friends. When you're out with people and you see your man in an argument with a friend of yours, don't turn it into a big incident.

Remember his Masculine Pretense. If you jump in and micromanage your man, he will soon start to feel emasculated. No man wants to feel that he needs a playground director to help him get along. For your man, expressing himself freely is a part of his need to travel light. If this means disagreeing strenuously with people in your life—with their values or points of view—then it has to be up to him. He has a lot more chance to get to like your friends if he can tell them what he really thinks.

WHEN HE DISLIKES A CLOSE FRIEND OF YOURS

The truly serious problems involving your friends arise mostly when your friends *aren't* in the room—when you and your man are alone and your friends are there only in spirit. Your friends become points of argument or *symbols* of problems between the two of you.

The most dangerous starting place is your man's expressing strong disapproval of some friend of yours. In the worst-case scenario, your man spent the evening with a friend of yours, which you thought went okay. On the surface, you saw nothing wrong. But the minute your man gets you alone, he surprises you with an attack on your friend. It's hard not to feel that your man is really attacking you.

Maybe he is, maybe he isn't. Probably he himself doesn't know yet—it's not decided. But what you do right now will prove very important.

Possibly your man has a point about your friend. Maybe she isn't always the most honest person, or she does tend to be negative about men. But you've decided long ago that she is worthwhile to know despite her faults. And you are certainly in no mood to reevaluate her now while your man is blasting her. In fact, you probably feel like jumping in and asking your man how dare he question your good friend.

But don't. Let him finish his case, as silly or accurate as it may be.

It may take almost superhuman effort to do this. But if you want to keep the lines of communication open with your man, you will have to.

Try to understand what's going on in your man's mind as he fixates on your friend. Almost surely, if he's carrying on this much, **he is secretly worried that you are like the friend.** There is only one way to assure him that you are on his side (whether or not you think he's going off the deep end), and that is to let him say what he needs to say. If you shut him up too soon, defend your friend before you've heard his full complaint, he will feel that you and your friend are together in an enemy camp.

Extreme? Of course. But that's the nature of the Masculine Pretense and his need to be number one with you. Later on you may choose to agree with some of what he says, or to disagree entirely. But right now, you have to let him see that you are loyal enough to hear him out and allow him to state his position fully.

If it's hard to listen without breaking in, remind yourself, **he has no right to judge me by another person, and if he loves me, he won't.** Remember that you have done nothing wrong. Hearing your man out, even if he's totally wrong, is the strongest way you can say, "Feel what you wish about that person. You aren't talking about me."

When he has finished, if you decide that your man is being totally unfair, say so. But possibly you'll agree with some of what he says. You may want to tell him that he has a point. True, your friend is very down on men, or maybe she did pay no attention to him all evening, or maybe she does ask for one favor after another. You agree that this was wrong, but she is your friend for a reason, and if your man respects you, he has to respect that reason.

You can certainly make some compromises with him. If he really dislikes the person, he shouldn't have to see as much of him or her as he has been. Of course, your man has no right to control how much you see your friend or how much you continue to like her. And he has absolutely no right to ask you to cut your friend out of your life. If he turns this into an ultimatum situation—her or me— you have to tell him he's going too far. You don't have to rearrange your friendships. It should be enough if you hear your man out, try to arrange a comfortable compromise, and let him know that when he feels injured, you care.

Brent, a man in his thirties who was a patient of mine, went with his new girlfriend, Jill, to a gallery opening in honor of a close woman friend of Jill's, a painter. At the gallery, the artist talked to Brent, doubtless considering him a prospective buyer. She talked about herself exclusively—which was fine with Brent. After all, it was her evening, not his. Brent bought one of her sketches.

Halfway through the evening, Jill's friend took Brent aside and suddenly began to lecture him. "Jill is very vulnerable," she began. "She went through a lot in her divorce. I hope you're the kind of man who takes care of women. We're all a little nervous that Jill has jumped into this relationship too fast, and we're hoping that you're not here just to take advantage of her."

Brent was so taken aback that he was nearly speechless. Naturally, he felt accused, on the spot, and under pressure. His Masculine Pretense took badly to the image of Jill's friends discussing him to decide if he was a "user" or a "provider." Jill had mentioned that her divorce was rocky, but she was far from a needy person. Brent had seen her as a strong, independent woman coming into this exciting, new relationship on her own terms.

During the next day, Brent found himself feeling increasingly annoyed at what he had come to see as an ambush. He told Jill how upset he'd felt. "That woman made me feel like a criminal, and she made you sound like a mess. Doesn't it upset you when it's so far from the truth?"

But Jill instantly accused Brent of being "oversensitive." "She was just trying to help," Jill snapped at Brent, in defense of her friend. "That's the way she is, always worrying about other people."

"Well, she certainly wasn't worrying about me," Brent said. "She didn't even act as if I was a person."

"Why should she?" Jill shot back. "I'm the one who has been her friend for ten years. She hadn't even heard of you a month ago."

The argument escalated, and things rapidly went from bad to worse.

A few days later, they came into my office together and sat on opposite ends of the couch. We pieced together what had happened. Jill was able to acknowledge that she had taken her friend's side before Brent had even finished his complaint. She had acted reflexively, treating Brent as if he were the enemy simply because he had expressed discontent. Brent was able to explain how bad the comment had made him feel. And not just for himself, but for Jill. Why should a friend portray Jill as a victim when it was so far from reality? Jill finally admitted that the remark bothered her too. "Obviously, I don't need a caretaker," she said. "Of course, I wish she hadn't said any of that." They were finally on the same page again.

When things softened between Brent and Jill, she volunteered that though she was close to her artist friend, they had always differed greatly on their view of male-female relationships. The woman was cynical about men and tended to treat them harshly. Jill had been aware of this but still felt an urge to defend this woman who had been kind to her in the past. The discussion brought Jill and Brent closer than ever. Afterward, Jill felt that she could be honest about the nuances of her friendships; she wouldn't have to defend her friends to the death against Brent. And Brent realized that Jill didn't embody the faults of all her friends. Compromises were made on both sides. Jill would speak up if a friend said something negative to Brent, and Brent would not demand that Jill banish people from her life just because he didn't like them.

WHAT YOU TELL HIM ABOUT YOUR FRIENDS

When you are behind closed doors with your man, you may be tempted to cuddle up to him by revealing secrets about your friends. Beware. Telling your man too much, too soon, about a friend can boomerang and cause you big trouble down the road.

You're in bed during a quiet interlude. You whisper to your man that a close woman friend of yours, whom he has met, is cheating on her husband. Or that a friend told you in confidence that her husband's business is failing and they're both desperate for money.

You know that your friend would be heartsick if she ever found out that you revealed her confidence, but you trust that your man will never let on. Probably he won't. But even as you speak, you'll probably feel that you are betraying your friend. For what? For an intimate moment with a man who is supposed to love you anyhow. Your man certainly won't think more of you for being a gossip; he's more likely to think less of you, and tell you less about himself. He may start wondering if you can be loyal to anyone.

Understand too that you can't always stop with a single disclosure. Maybe your man will be fascinated by your friend's secret love affair and want to know all the details. You'll find yourself telling him much more than you intended. When, months later, your man asks you how your friend's love affair is progressing, you won't be happy—especially if things aren't going so well with your man at the time. You'll feel as if you sold important state secrets to the enemy. Worse than that, you *gave* them away so that the enemy would like you.

And, of course, once you reveal information, you can't take it back. Your man can use it as he will, so long as he keeps it a secret.

Suppose he has an argument with your friend's husband. Now, alone with you, he doesn't just run the guy down, he uses *your information* to run him down. "That guy's a real idiot. No wonder his business is going under. Did you hear what he said?" You'll probably want to disappear through the floorboards. You could have avoided the whole problem by not revealing your friend's trusted secret.

The time may come when you can tell your man everything, but almost surely that time hasn't come yet. And you can't hurry it along.

DISCUSSING YOUR MAN WITH YOUR FRIENDS

Before you met this man and probably after your first few dates, you may have told your friends every detail of your romantic hopes and expectations. You perhaps asked them for their analyses and took their advice seriously. As you and your man become closer, you may be tempted to keep up this steady exchange of information about him. But look out. What you say to your friends about him can come back to haunt you.

There is magic in growing together with your man, becoming closer, making mistakes, learning secrets about each other. This is the magic of love, with all its intensity, its exaggeration, its uncertainty, and its conspiracy. At best, you and your man have the sense that no one has ever been here before, which is true in the respect that you two were never here before together and have no precedent.

You can't possibly reach this pinnacle, this nameless magic that makes marriage a mere confirmation, if you go on discussing every detail of your romance with friends. Just as you should be wary about telling your man too much about your friends, be careful about telling too many people play-by-play, intimate details of your relationship. It's one thing if you are in trouble and really need help, but don't lapse into the habit of revealing intimacies just to brag, chat, or entertain your friends. You may have been using your friends to keep you afloat between relationships and as this one was getting started. Now you may feel that you are being unfair because you sense that the time has come to keep things private and tell them less. But good friends will intuitively understand that as things get serious between you and your man, the details of your life take on special meaning and can't always be shared so easily.

This is also important for another reason. Oddly enough, your man will have a strange, startlingly intuitive sense of when you are revealing too much personal data of his to your friends. Because of his Masculine Pretense (which is always accompanied by a touch of paranoia), he is acutely frightened of being witnessed or judged.

Several times men have come into my office and said, seemingly a propos of nothing, "I think she's discussing me with people." When I ask them why, they find it hard to answer at first. Then they identify some subtle change in the woman's behavior, as if she's been told to "handle" him differently, and the man sees what he considers artificiality. The change might be as subtle as her not being as free and immediate as usual, or as her suddenly pressing the man to do something as if it's a benchmark or a point of honor. Out of the blue, she is obsessed about his joining her family for Thanksgiving or going with her to her high school reunion.

The man feels that this sudden demand represents a network of support. He can practically hear the woman's friends insisting, "If he loves you, he'll do this for you." He is far more troubled by the idea that his relationship is being discussed and dissected by other people than by anything that the woman is asking for.

If you really want to make your friends hideous intruders into your love life, just quote them in an argument: "Most of the people at the party thought that you were awfully quiet. They wondered if there was something wrong." Or use them as leverage: "Jan and

Rick are going to a bed-and-breakfast for a week this fall. And Melissa and her boyfriend are going to the Bahamas. They don't really understand why you won't go away with me."

Don't let your unseen friends in the background mess up your love affair. If you want something, it should be because *you* want it. If you feel something, it should be because *you* feel it, not because your friends advise it. Your friends are a great source of enrichment to you, and maybe to your man. Let that role suffice. Don't invite them in too close by pressing them on his psyche.

ENTERING YOUR MAN'S WORLD

Your man is much more alone in the world than you are. At most, he probably has one or two close friends, and even they aren't intimate in the ways that you are with your woman friends. His bond with those friends probably consists largely of shared interests. He and his friends have nothing like the daily follow-up and continuity that you have with your friends. His buddy, Todd, doesn't call to ask how that chat with his boss went last week or if he's having fun wearing that expensive leather jacket he splurged on. As we've seen, most men don't "waste time" talking about their feelings. In fact, his friends wouldn't think twice about it if he disappeared entirely for stretches of time.

Men talk mostly about objective things. Your man may discuss stocks with his friends, or ask them if they're going to the game tonight or going fishing, or if they saw Tiger Woods on Sunday. Questions like "How's business?" or "How's the family?" are likely to be more ritualistic than real. Men mostly *do* things with each other, like going to a favorite restaurant, playing tennis, or going to concerts when particular performers are in town. You'll probably meet his friends in some casual way. If others in his group are bringing dates somewhere, he'll want you to go with him.

It's not uncommon for a man to introduce his new woman to friends without having told them anything about her—even that she exists: "By the way, I'll be coming with Jane." "Who's Jane?" "Oh, she's someone I've been seeing for a couple of months." "No problem. How's eight o'clock?" "Good." Your man might participate in this dialogue even if he's madly in love with you. It's just that in the early stages men tend not to integrate romance with the rest of their lives the way women do. But, as we've seen, your man's present life doesn't truly fulfill him. He feels deeply that something is missing— a woman with whom he can be intimate and share his experiences. He secretly wants you with him as he moves through social situations and faces new challenges. But his Masculine Pretense inhibits him, and it's hard for him to bring you in. To his friends, he is a free spirit. It's hard for him to suddenly change his role in their eyes and start presenting himself as part of a couple.

And there's another issue. Your man may be afraid of declaring his commitment to you by bringing you everywhere and letting the world see how important you are to him. He knows that once you are seen with him repeatedly, the stakes will go up. After a while, people may expect him to marry you, and even now after they meet you, they will start expecting you to join him in many social situations.

But no matter how difficult it is for your man to make the transition, **you have to insist on participating in his social life.** If he hasn't made a move to introduce you to anyone after a reasonable period of time (say, six dates), make a fuss. This is one of those times when you *have* to challenge his need to travel light early on. If you don't, your romance will be all over before it starts. Not only is it hurtful to you to be excluded. By leaving you out, your man is also reinforcing his fear of integrating you into his life. He won't think more of you, he'll think *less* of you if he doesn't bring you into the mainstream.

Men don't marry women that they keep in the shadows. They marry the woman who *belongs* in their social circle, and the only way you can prove you belong there is to insist on being there. If you don't, some other woman will. By insisting, you are telling your man that you are a real candidate for marriage, and he had better see you that way. Do this, and his Masculine Pretense will start to work in your favor. He will want to show everyone that he can assume full possession of this woman—namely, you—whom his friends already know and like.

The flip side is that if he absolutely refuses to present you to the people who matter in his life, he's definitely not thinking in terms of marriage. It's better to discover this painful fact now and move on than to discover it later on when you care about him even more.

You may feel nervous before meeting his friends, especially if he's been telling you how great they are. But remind yourself that, just as he won't like all your friends, you won't like all of his. We learned in geometry that things equal to the same thing are equal to each other, but this doesn't hold true for relationships. They're much too complex. Keeping this in mind will take a lot of the pressure off.

Being with the people in his life is not a command performance. You're not on trial. Take comfort in realizing that his friends are probably not going to give him evaluations of you anyhow. Men don't usually offer unsolicited critiques to their men friends beyond saying "She's nice" or "She's pretty." They aren't that concerned with whom your man spends his time. It would take a serious clash of personalities for one of his friends to interfere.

Not only won't his men friends talk about you after you meet them. They probably won't talk to him *at all* about anything until something comes up of interest to them both. Men don't call each other after events and dissect them the way women do. Compared with women, men are much more forward looking than backward looking, a difference that has advantages and disadvantages.

Think about meeting his friends the way you thought about our first date. Your primary aim should be to stay loose and have a good time. Much of the other advice for the first date holds. Ask people questions but stay away from asking them about their résumés. Enjoy the people you meet as much as you can.

Try to connect with everyone, but realize that if a friend of his has a complex reaction to you, there may be little you can do about it. Maybe somebody finds it hard to accept you because he or she felt comfortable with your man's last girlfriend. You can't help that. You're not a replacement. If someone in the room wants your man's deceased wife to be reborn or doesn't like your religion or social status, this isn't your problem.

Again, remind yourself of the following mantra: **Nothing that your man's friends can possibly do or say about you can matter unless he sees things the way they do.** If your man is a wimp who turns against you because friends of his don't like you, there's nothing you can do. And why would you want to?

One pitfall needs special mention. If one of the new people that you meet does decide to give you a hard time, you have every right to protect yourself. But try as hard as you can to do this without putting your man in the middle. Don't make him fight your battles for you. Nothing will destroy your man's sense of traveling light faster than having to choose sides between you and his old friends.

Women patients of mine have often described being subjected to surprise attacks by one of their man's friends. Nine out of ten times it's *another woman* who attacks them. You'll find that your man's men friends have little stake in whether he sees you or not. But beware of any long-standing woman friend of your man's who feels possessive toward him. (She's likely to be the woman who whispers to you about what he likes and dislikes, or refers to past adventures they've had together. She acts as if she owns the guy.) Whether or not this female nemesis wanted your man for herself or it's just her nature to compete with very woman she meets doesn't matter. The bottom line is the same. She wants you to disappear.

My patient Pat was thrown completely off balance when a woman friend of her boyfriend, Brian, commented to her, "I guess I'll see you again on Thanksgiving weekend if you're still together." Pat was stunned and a moment later infuriated by the remark. But afraid that she'd say something terrible and unforgettable, she said nothing at all. She just simmered.

That night, when Pat was alone with Brian, she was unable to contain herself further. She confronted him, as if *he* were the one who had undermined her. "Don't deny it," she said in a rage. "You must have given that bitch the impression that I might not be here in two months." She shouted at Brian, "You better tell her that you're serious about me," and she thrust the phone in his hand.

Brian didn't make the call. It was two in the morning, and the next day things calmed down. But Pat had definitely set the relationship back by putting Brian on the spot when she herself hadn't known what to do. For at least a few days, Brian must have wished that he'd never brought Pat into his circle at all.

It's human nature to feel stung when you are attacked. But if you run to your man and ask him to defend you, you are playing right into the assailant's hands. Your nemesis wants to divide you but won't be able to if you keep your cool. Anyone can say something nasty to us and blindside us, that's easy. And very few of us are witty or verbal enough to immediately come up with the perfect, devastating reply. Forgive yourself if you can't do this.

But don't let yourself be defeated either. You don't have to walk away without doing anything.

As a therapist, I recommend a simple technique for dealing with veiled insults. Just keep asking the person who made the comment to *clarify*. The aggressor says, "We'll see you on Thanksgiving if you're still together." Ask quietly for clarification. "What do you mean, *'if* we're still together?' " This forces the person to provide some sort of explanation. "Well, Brian never stays with women very long."

Even your first question brings the person's malice more into the open. And don't stop here. Ask for more clarity. "Are you telling me that Brian is going to leave me for sure? How do you know?" By now the other person will be sorry he or she spoke at all. Your nemesis will probably back away, say that the whole thing was a misunderstanding, let it go, and learn the valuable lesson to leave you alone. If you can't be pushed around, it's not worth the trouble to the other person.

You aren't being combative. You are simply *drawing the other person out*, forcing him or her to put this ugly innuendo into plain language so everyone can see it. If Pat had done this, Brian would have seen what was really going on. She would have shed light on the other woman's hostility toward her, and shown that she was a competent person who could take care of herself and let her man travel light.

After using this technique, if you choose to discuss the interaction later with your man, you can do it lightly. Then if your man says, "I can't understand why she said that. Do you want me to bring it up with her?" you can reply quietly, "Oh, no, that's not necessary. It's been taken care of."

BALANCING ROMANCE WITH FRIENDSHIP

When your romance is in its first bloom, you and your man will probably withdraw somewhat from the outside world. Why spend time with friends when it's so much better to be alone with each other! Your friends and his are still in the picture, but more in the background. You don't turn to them as often as you did for their support, or for intimacy, or to help you feel special. You have each other.

As you step back from the world, you may start to see that some of the people on the periphery of your life weren't truly friends at all. They were people with whom you killed time—the person you never really liked but who kept you company during your dark hours, the one who criticized you regularly and wasn't rooting for you but who got you invited places, the friend who hates men and would surely find fault with this relationship, the depressive whom you felt sorry for. Many of these people will end up gone forever.

But after some months or perhaps a year, both you and your man will come to a second stage when you seriously miss a few really close friends whom you haven't been seeing enough of. No matter how much you love each other, you can't fulfill each other's needs completely. You'll remember special things that you got from certain individuals and yearn to reconnect with them. You will both crave outside stimulation and start to worry that maybe you excluded some of your friends too abruptly when you fell in love.

You'll pursue these friends again, hoping that they'll accept you back, and they probably will. Most men won't mind it when you resume relationships with your old friends. Once your man feels secure in your love, he'll hardly notice. He's not threatened by your friends if he knows he's numero uno.

It's more frequently the woman who panics when her man decides to take time away from the romance and spend it with others. It can be scary because it looks like a regression to his life before you came along. You can't help worrying that he's getting tired of you—falling out of love rather than moving toward commitment.

But more likely he's just yearning for certain affirmations of his masculinity that he has always relied on.

Sure, *you* are the ultimate proof of his masculinity. But just as you did, he got certain "emotional supplies" from particular individuals in his life. Maybe you have one special friend who always says just the right thing about business issues, another whom you can have lunch with and be giddy and talk about shoes, and another who loves to go into the nitty-gritty of people's personalities. These people all enable you to express different facets of your nature. It's the same for him. He needs men to talk "guy talk" with, or to play a serious game of tennis with, or to be a wise guy with—to affirm his masculinity with them as he always has.

When he mentions doing a few things with his friends over a weekend, your challenge is not to look as if you're falling apart. Above all, don't imply that your man is betraying you. Don't hit him with self-pity. Leave the "poor me" routine out of the equation: "Don't you still love me?" "I'm *so* disappointed." "But we're always together on Saturday mornings."

Why imply that he promised to banish the world and to spend his life with you alone? He didn't make that promise, and even if he did, he can't possibly keep it. If you make it a "me or them" situation, you are challenging his need to travel light in a way that no man can accept. You couldn't accept it either. No lover is worth rejecting the whole world.

Once you grasp that your man needs supplies from you *and* from other people, you won't be nearly as stressed. Before you, he had his buddies, but no romance. Then, for a while, romance was enough. He had accumulated enough from his friendships to survive for a while without them. But his need to replenish them kept growing, and now it is surfacing.

Don't make this a competition for his affections between you and others. Real intimacy doesn't cling. His return to his old friends is one of the first major tests of your willingness to let him travel light. If you pass it, you will be giving him a great gift.

Your misgivings—or jealousy—will pass as you realize that he's not resuming a rogue male pattern. He's just acting like a normal person who is lucky enough to have friends. Welcome his coming and going, within reason (as, of course, he should welcome yours), and he'll realize that his romance with you can breathe and can go the distance. Each time he leaves and comes back, your love affair will be stronger than ever.

Your own friends will probably be glad to see more of you, and most will probably be positive about your relationship. But how do you handle it if you learn that one of your women friends is dead set against your new man? You certainly owe it to her to listen to her objection. Maybe she has seen something that you've missed or that you have sensed keenly but been trying to deny to yourself. Don't let love blind you entirely to input from others.

But remember that this relationship is yours and in your hands. Recommendations from other people shouldn't matter if you are happy. Often a friend will give you advice based on the person you used to be. "But how can you marry a schoolteacher when you always said that money was so important to you?" "But you said you never wanted kids." Maybe your values or interests have changed since you met this man. No friend has the right to freeze you as the person you once were.

You and your man have probably both changed since you met. Your new goals have a little of each of you in them, and anyone who respects you should understand this.

Your friends can enrich your life in a multitude of ways. Their perceptions can often broaden yours, but in the end you must make the major decisions about your life. And of all the decisions you make, none is more important than your choice of the man you marry.

PART THREE

Taking Care of Yourself

8

How to Argue with a Lover

Up until now, we've been talking extensively about your man's needs. Your aim has been to get through to him in a way that no other woman has, and to create the right atmosphere for a relationship to grow. But obviously you can't spend a lifetime catering to your man. You have needs too, and you owe it to yourself to fulfill them with the same intensity that you devote to him.

As your relationship settles in and becomes real, you will inevitably find places where you and your man differ in outlook or in preference. Even two people in love, who want the same things in life, can be oblivious to each other's needs at times. When this happens, the person who is feeling deprived has to speak up. If this person happens to be you, you will have to take a position and assert it. Unless you stand up for yourself early, and perhaps repeatedly, deprivations can cause real trouble.

It may seem daunting to confront a man who is wearing the armor of Masculine Pretense. His first reaction to any challenge may be to feel threatened, act tough, and not listen. For just this reason—because men can appear so formidable—women too often twist themselves out of shape in order to avoid anything that might look like a confrontation. They limit themselves once they get into a serious relationship much more than they have to.

You've very possibly been so busy studying your man and trying to give him what he wants that you've lost touch with at least some of your own needs. Let's face it, women tend to compromise much more than men do anyhow.

Look at any relationship and you'll see that it is usually the woman who makes the big concessions so that things will go smoothly. It's most often the woman who gives up her apartment when they move in together. It's more often the woman who gives up time-consuming interests so that the two of them can be together more. She will arrange her vacations to match his more often than the other way around.

In fact, many women will often do nearly anything to avoid confrontations with their man. This may include lying. It may seem easier to go underground and simply avoid dealing with your man on certain issues. When he asks you who you had lunch with, you blurt out, "My friend Julie," instead of telling him that you took your ex-boyfriend, Bob, out for his annual birthday lunch. You've been doing it for ten years and you know that it's completely innocent. Bob is happily married, and you can't even remember a time when you were attracted to him. The two of you are loyal friends, and you really don't want to explain yourself to this new man, who may be jealous and skittish when other males are in the picture.

But subterfuge is always self-defeating. Obviously if you lie, you risk getting caught, and with his profound loyalty need, this guy may feel terribly betrayed. Your explanation that you lied because he backed you into a corner will fall on deaf ears. He will feel self-righteous and may even punish you over time.

Try to avoid lying, as well as overcompromising, because either way you are introducing a terrible pessimism into the relationship. In a sense, doing either is a form of giving up on the romance as an open, loving exchange. In deciding not to tell your man what you really feel, what you really *want*, you are saying in effect, "I don't trust you and I am *afraid* of you."

You know that the romance you always had in mind before you met this man was honest and open. You pictured a relationship where you could each talk freely about what you needed. Be true to this dream. Make clear your wants as confidently as you would if you weren't afraid of losing him.

Don't condemn the guy by assuming in advance that he'll try to prevent you from living as you choose. And don't assume that he's unwilling to correct anything in his own behavior. Many a woman who has settled for a life of silent resentment and self-sacrifice could have had infinitely more if she trusted herself, and trusted her man enough, to take more—and, if necessary, to argue for it.

Your man may seem difficult at times, but he's probably not hopeless. Though his Masculine Pretense can make him brittle and oversensitive, it doesn't utterly cloud his reasoning. He lives in the real world and retains some glimmer of what fair play is.

If this relationship is to live, it has got to breathe. And it can breathe only if you are *both* breathing, which requires that you get the oxygen you need. Even as you concentrate on his needs, concentrate on your own too. Pursue what you want directly, not in roundabout ways, and the commitment that you are working toward will be fulfilling for both of you.

YOU DON'T NEED YOUR MAN'S PERMISSION TO LIVE

Before you met this man, you made independent decisions every day and acted on them. When your decisions involved other peo-

ple, you discussed them. Maybe you and a woman friend decided
to share expenses on a summer rental, so you looked at places together and weighed their cost. You didn't ask your friend if it was
okay to rent a cottage for summer weekends; you only asked her if
she wanted to join you. Even when you sought someone's advice—
their opinion about a job that you were considering, or if a certain
outfit was right for an event—you weren't asking the person for
permission to take the job or wear the pantsuit. You were collect-
ing data to help you decide what to do.

This is the way it should be with your man.

Don't start asking him for permission to do things that you want
to do. Your man is at most your equal, not your superior or judge.
You may want his input, but you shouldn't have to persuade him
that what you want is fair and valid, any more than he should have
to persuade you that it's okay to watch the World Series.

A great many women fall into the pattern of seeing their man as
the main decision maker. Right from the start, they concede this
role to their man, as if it's his birthright, even if he has proven himself far *less* competent in the world than they are. They enslave
themselves because they think the relationship is more important to
them than it is to their man. They live with the repeated picture of
their man being angry for days or walking out if they do something
that displeases him.

Avoid this mistake, which is based both on fear of your man and
a lack of respect for yourself. We have seen that, as part of his
Masculine Pretense, your man may present himself as someone who
can walk out at any moment—he hides his need for intimacy and
talks about valuing freedom. But you know the real truth: he needs
you every bit as much as you need him. If you are hanging on to this
relationship by your thumbs, and compromising your own needs,
you are cheating yourself out of a life and probably out of the relationship.

Unless this guy is a hopeless jerk, the woman he really wants isn't someone who dotes on him and waits for instructions. She is someone with a mind of her own and with the courage of her own opinions.

MAKE THE SAME KINDS OF DECISIONS THAT YOU'VE ALWAYS MADE

You can avoid a lot of arguments by simply living your life, lovingly with him, and sometimes happily without him. Many things that he's not used to won't seem strange to him if you simply do them in stride. Obviously he has a right to know when you're not going to be around or when people are entering his life, or his home. But it's your life too, or your home, and the best way for him to learn about a relationship is to see how one works.

Instead of asking your man's permission to live, simply do the things you want to do. Unless they directly concern him, you are always better off making your own decisions and then acting on them. Maybe he won't be thrilled about your joining the office softball team and coming home late a few nights a week. But if you really love to play and enjoy the camaraderie, this isn't something you should need permission to do. Tell him that you are signing up, and then sign up. Assume that if he sees how much fun it is for you, he won't go crazy. He can even use the time when you're away to catch up with his friends, his work, or his sleep.

You know which acts are treasonous and which aren't. If in your opinion what you want to do is reasonable, then just do it. Don't assume that he'll go berserk. If you had regular dinners with your ex-husband to discuss your kid, keep having them. If he complains about the dinners, be sensitive to his feelings and hear him out. If he's reasonable, you can certainly tell him what you talked about. But you aren't going to stop regular communication with your child's father. If you spent a certain amount on clothes or luxuries, keep spending it. If you planned to host certain events at your apartment, go ahead and arrange them.

Inform your man of whatever you consider necessary for your happiness. If he has a big problem with something that you are doing or plan to do, he owes you an honest, open explanation of why he objects. And he needs to make clear that he sees exactly what's at stake for you.

Women who make men their bosses are every bit as responsible for the imbalance as their men are. Being in a romantic relationship doesn't mean that you have to give up your autonomy.

ARGUING 101

But what if your man tries to pull imaginary rank and act as if he's your superior? "If we are going to live together, you can't possibly spend that much money on a hair salon every month." Or, "Why do you have to be the last one to leave your office every night? You're in a relationship. We have enough money without your getting more promotions."

Obviously, when your man protests something that you are doing or want to do, you have to stand up for yourself. And you have to speak loudly and clearly if he keeps doing something hurtful to you or self-destructive.

Arguing with loved ones is part of life. The important thing is to know *how* to argue so that you keep the argument contained and relevant. Knowing how to argue will enable you to avoid the kinds of hurtful comments that threaten a relationship.

As you must have experienced already, emotions run very high in a love affair. Getting through to your man is more difficult because of his Masculine Pretense, which can make him rigid and oversensitive. He may be quick to see disloyalty in you when you are merely insisting on a basic right or doing what you always did. Your man's infantile need to feel special can make him unfairly demanding until he sees the light.

But his weakness shouldn't discourage you from taking a position on your own behalf when you feel it is proper. And if you know how to argue, you can usually overcome even the obstacle of his Masculine Pretense.

The best way to understand how to argue is to start out by considering what an argument is *not*. The aim of an argument is not to humiliate the other person. It isn't to get the person to apologize for twenty other things that he or she did to you, to admit that he or she has mistreated you for the last how many months or years, to wreak vengeance on the person for a lot of things that have been secretly bothering you, or to force the person to embark on a broad program of behavioral improvement.

Nor is the aim of an argument to make a person feel so guilty or sorry that he showers you with gifts and repeated apologies for the coming month.

If you feel that you want these things, then you don't need this chapter on how to argue. There's a deep problem in your relationship, or at least you feel that there is. It's bigger than any single issue that you might want to argue about and resolve. Some major trend in the relationship is upsetting you, and you need to look at the next chapter, which can give you some insights if the trouble gets this serious.

An argument is—or ought to be—a discussion in which you attempt to convince another person of some single point. The two basic rules for arguing can be summed up in the following strategy: stay friends with the other person's unconscious. You want to win your point without inflaming the other person or starting a war. This holds for *any argument*, not just one that you might have with your man.

The two rules for staying friends with the other person's unconscious are based on certain eternal truths of human nature:

1.   People need to like themselves, whether they are right or wrong.
2.   People need to feel consistent.

If you think about it, you can see that both of these points are intuitively true.

Think first about our need to like ourselves. Imagine that you had a big blowup with a close woman friend. She accused you of revealing a confidence, but you didn't actually do it. Her accusation is bad enough, but how much worse would it be if she added, "You *always* had a big mouth, and you just don't care how other people feel." Your friend would be telling you not to like yourself anymore. This would be a sweeping character damnation; it could end a friendship.

And suppose you did blurt out the confidence unthinkingly. You already feel horrible. If you apologize and assure your friend that you'll never slip again, she has two options. Either to go on complaining about the damage you did and make you hate yourself more. Or accept your apology graciously and agree: "I realize that you weren't trying to hurt me." If she continues on the first track, she'll make you dislike yourself, and soon you will start to resent her. Self-hatred nearly always turns into hatred of the accuser.

If the friend allows you to walk away *liking yourself,* feeling that you are still a decent person and a good friend, you can also go on liking her. She has made her point, but even more strongly, because now you care. You will remain her friend and be more careful about confidences in the future. The same holds true with your man. Allow him to go on liking himself as you make your point.

The second rule—that of *consistency*—follows from the first and is just as important. People will always adjust data so that they come out looking logical and consistent to themselves. We all need to feel that we've been sane and reasonable in the past. This is why it is very wrong to resort to attacking someone's character or to make any sweeping accusations when arguing. When we're hurt, we have the impulse to say, "I'm going to make this person see how utterly rotten he's been. Then he'll be sorry, and treat me better."

Amazingly, because of the rule of consistency, **the tactic of trying to make the other person feel guilt or pity always backfires.** Trying to show someone that he has always been unfair is the worst thing you can do in an argument.

When you want a raise, you may feel like telling your boss that he's cheap, that he's always underpaid you, and that he didn't even notice all the extra work you did this year. You picture him saying, "Oh, you're right. I've been thoughtless. Now I realize what a big asset you are. How can I make it up to you?" But things work exactly the opposite way. When you tell your boss that he's been unfair to you over time, he won't see you as an abused victim and himself as a monster. Don't forget, he needs to like himself. What he'll do is try to adjust the data so that he comes out as a good guy and a consistent person.

Instead of readjusting his thinking along your lines, he'll reason something like this. "She's absolutely right. I *have* been paying her less than other people. And now I remember *why.*" He'll start making a case in his mind so that he can go on feeling consistent as well as decent. "I've been paying her less because she isn't a college graduate." Or, "Because she complains a lot." Or, "Because she made a big mistake last year."

Before you backed your boss into a corner, he might not have considered any of these things important, but you have forced him to justify to himself the way he has treated you. You have driven him to find a reason, and he won't be satisfied until he finds one that makes him look like a decent person. Naturally, he'd rather like himself than feel guilty every time he sees you.

You have to keep people happy with themselves if you want them to see things your way. Otherwise, even if you get your way, you weaken the relationship. You certainly don't want to do this with the man you hope to spend your life with.

RESPECTING HIS NEEDS WHILE UNDER FIRE

Respecting your man's four basic needs is as important during an argument as at any other time. Maybe even more so. But during a dispute, it's a lot harder to do. Obviously, it is during arguments, when passions run high, that people say things that can cause lasting trouble. When you're in pain, you may want to fire your biggest guns and do whatever damage you can—anything to show this guy that he can't push you around. It's because you may feel so helpless that you want to go for the jugular. We all know that arguments between lovers can get incendiary and escalate out of all proportion. When this happens, the real problems that arise almost never involve the original dispute.

You've probably had at least one argument with a man who stunned you by his viciousness. He went much too far and revealed a whole vision of you that you didn't recover from—at least not for a long time. Obviously, if your man does this in an argument—if, for instance, he compares you unfavorably with another woman, or attacks your basic integrity—you would be better off not talking to him at all until he calms down. This doesn't mean that you are putting your point aside, only that you are going to make it later. You may also want to talk to him about his use of overkill.

But don't you make the same mistake of overgeneralizing.

The key to being effective in arguing with your man is: **Stay relevant and never withdraw support for any of his four basic needs.**

Not only is he most apt to see the light if you do this. You can actually improve your romance by showing how much you care for your man even at a time when you are very hurt or angry at him.

Of course, you won't be sharply conscious of his needs when you are furious at him. That would be asking too much of any mortal. But if you follow certain guidelines, you'll say the right things even under fire.

Let's look at these guidelines for arguing with your man. If you keep within them, your case will be strong, and after the argument, the two of you may well feel closer rather than further apart.

MAKE HIM FEEL SPECIAL EVEN DURING AN ARGUMENT

You know how much you want to feel special to your man. You could take nearly any request or complaint in stride so long as he kept seeing you as the *unique* woman in his life, incomparable with others. On the other hand, if he told you during an argument that you were just like every other women he has known, you would feel crushed.

As we've seen, your man's need to feel special is even greater than yours. He'll see your point more readily if he can go on feeling special to you during your argument. And remember your man's need to like himself and to feel consistent.

You can often make your point by helping your man see that he is bigger than whatever you are arguing about. For example, if your lover irrationally objects to your taking your old boyfriend Bob out for his birthday, try making your case in a positive way. Remind your man that he isn't ordinarily a jealous or controlling person, which is one reason you love him so much. Reassure him that he is special. Tell him again that he has no reason on earth to worry about any other man.

*   *   *

If you need to go on with your argument, keep other people out of it. **Never compare your man unfavorably with other men as a device to make a point.** Comparisons rob him of his specialness. Your intention may be to shame him by mentioning another guy. But every such mention sets that guy up as a rival and diminishes your man's feeling that you see him as special and beyond compare.

You know how horrible you would feel if he compared you unfavorably with another woman. "Why can't you be as self-confident as Sarah?" Your man will feel at least as bad if you do this to him. Even if he does what you want, your comparison will cost you intimacy and trust.

Let's say that you want him to change his Saturday plans so that he can help you do some shopping. Some of his friends are coming over later, and they will need snacks. You have a strong case: you worked all week, just as he did, and you shouldn't have to do the shopping alone, especially since they're his friends. You'd like to have some time for yourself, and if he helped you, things would go faster and you could both cut out for a few hours.

Say all this but *avoid comparisons.* Stay away from: "Joe shares all the chores with Ellen." Or, "Gary is never unfair to Diana." Resist your impulse to use other men as exemplars. Your man isn't in some race to be more attentive or better than anyone else. Nearly always, your reason for bringing other people into an argument is that you fear that your case is weak or that your man is unreasonable. You are using an army because you feel that your own plea, based on your own worth, won't prevail. Once again, however, you have to trust your own fairness and trust that your man cares for you enough to be fair himself. You know that it's only right for him to help you bring in provisions for his friends. Talk to him as you would to a woman friend. "I'm happy to help you set up everything for your guests, but you need to help me at the store." Your man will probably go along. If he doesn't, base your subsequent case on the assumption that he's a fair person. "We've always counted on each other. Let's divide up the labor today as we always do." His going along this time allows him to feel consistent with the fair person he's always been. He can like himself and like you.

No matter how supportive you are of your man, however, the time will inevitably come when you feel that he is doing something hurtful to you or hurtful to himself. You will have to venture a criticism. The big rule here is to **make your suggestion as specific as you can.**

Once again, don't generalize. If he's impossibly sloppy and you spend half your time picking up after him, you have a right to ask him to be neater. Try not to expand, no matter how annoyed you are. Avoid, "You're sloppy about every detail in your life. No wonder your boss is always yelling at you." Or, "This shows what you really think of women. You see us all as maids."

A step worse than generalizing would be delving into your man's motives and telling him why he's really acting so badly. Doing this deprives him of all sense of specialness, and makes him look like an open book. "You treat women like this because your mother let you get away with everything. Now you want to turn me into a mother who has nothing else to do but take care of you."

Interpretations like these may come to mind at times. But when they do, keep them to yourself. No one wants to feel that you can see right through him. Your man, with his Masculine Pretense, needs to look utterly in command—not ordinary or transparent.

Be especially careful when your man comes to you for advice. When *you* ask someone for input, you don't want a long speech about how you messed up in three different areas, or how you always mess up. Your man dreads this even more because of his Masculine Pretense. His fear of being unmasked, of being seen as less than perfect, is what may have prevented him from coming to you for advice in the first place. Don't utilize his vulnerability as a chance to lecture him on what he's been doing wrong and how he can improve.

If you want to continue having input into your man's life, treasure those moments when he feels free enough to ask you for your opinion. Use these chances to make him feel closer to you—to establish yourself as a trustworthy friend.

Dan, a new writer for a major magazine, started a romance with Laura, who was a few years older and an established editor in a publishing company. Dan, who suffered frequent writer's block, would show his articles to Laura, and she spent several weekends finishing pieces for Dan and in one case saving his job. Soon Laura was picking subjects for Dan to write about and telling him how to handle people at work. The relationship was changing fast. Dan stopped being affectionate toward Laura, and she came to my office to find out what was going wrong.

Laura told me that she thought Dan could do a lot better at work if he disciplined himself more and became less self-indulgent as a writer. It came out that Laura had already said this to Dan quite bluntly. Dan had leaned on Laura in moments of uncertainty, and she had taken the opportunity to register fierce criticism of his whole approach to writing.

In therapy, Laura started to see that Dan was moving away from her emotionally. She realized that she never complimented him anymore; this was sad, because in the beginning she had told Dan what she truly felt, that he was a wonderful writer. When this came out, Laura at first defended herself. "What good is it if I just keep telling him how great he is? He asked my opinion, so I owe it to him to give it." This was true from Laura's point of view, but "constructive criticisms," if they break our spirit, do more harm than good.

At Laura's request, Dan came in to provide his version. He told me that he was losing all sexual feeling for Laura. He couldn't love a woman who was as corrective as his own mother. Of course his reaction wasn't truly fair, since he did depend on Laura so much. Poor Laura was giving up weekends to do whatever Dan asked her to do and yet, ironically, was in the process of destroying his love for her.

The only way to save their relationship was for Laura to stop volunteering suggestions, to back off her program of "improving Dan." In turn, Dan agreed that he'd try not to use Laura as a resource. He would certainly ask her opinions from time to time, but he would leave it at that. Laura promised to answer questions specifically, and to avoid generalizations. They would try to resume their relationship as lovers and no longer relate to each other as expert and student, which was killing them.

Whether you are making a case for something that you want to do or trying to help your man improve his life, you will be much more successful if you keep in mind his need to feel special.

ARGUING AND YOUR MAN'S NEED TO TRAVEL LIGHT

During an argument with a lover nearly all of us have sometimes felt: "Life was a lot easier when I didn't have to think about all this stuff." Men typically feel this more because of their neurotic need to feel completely unencumbered, as part of their Masculine Pretense.

The simple truth is that *every* relationship makes demands. If you want to travel completely light, you had better live alone. You can buy whatever car you want, you have sole power over the TV remote, and you never get home too late because nobody's waiting for you. In the end, it is up to the individual to decide if any relationship is worth the obligations that go with it. Once you start becoming a couple, you'll both have some restrictions; that's just part of living. Obviously, you are going to do things that displease him, and if he can't always travel as light as he did when he was alone, that's just his tough luck. You are going to argue with him at times, and sometimes you are going to ask him to act differently for your sake—or for his own.

If he has any power of reflection, your man should realize that arguments are part of intimacy. He will know that it's better to argue with someone you love at two in the morning than to be alone. I've had many men in my office realize this long after their marriages broke up. It's also better to argue than to have a loved one so afraid of you that she suffers in silence.

It's even better to have a loved one ask you an annoying number of questions about your day than to have no one care.

Three men friends and I were driving back from the tennis courts one afternoon. One of the men, who had been married for about thirty years, spoke briefly over his cell phone to his wife. They seemed to be arguing mildly. Afterward, the man turned to us and said, shaking his head, " 'What did I have for *lunch?'* she asked me. 'A sandwich,' I told her. 'What *kind* of sandwich?' she asked me. Women really are something."

There was a brief silence, after which another man observed, "Richard, where would you be if no one asked you what you had for lunch?"

I thought that the point was brilliantly made.

Don't worry about intruding once in a while. Err in the direction of asking too many questions or arguing, rather than going dead. Your man may have some misgivings about traveling light when you don't see eye to eye. But the occasional pressures and disagreements that accompany love and caring are a small price for him to pay to have someone who does care.

*   *   *

Even so, if you want your man to go along with your argument, it is important to make clear that you aren't asking him to give up life as he knew it. You will be most persuasive if he sees that even if he makes some adjustments, he can still travel light. The key is to ask for particular changes, but not whole swarms of them at once.

Never make more than one criticism at a time. Maybe you want your man to dress differently. You feel sure that he would come across better everywhere, and you would feel more proud of him if he did. Secretly, you'd like him to empty out his closet and go shopping with you for three straight days. But you are only allowed one comment at a time. If you have a suggestion about the kind of shoes he'd look great in, make it. And leave it at that. If you want him to stop wearing T-shirts when he meets clients on the weekends, mention this gently, and then leave it alone.

Your man will probably tolerate a single enhancement here and there, but a sweeping self-improvement program will activate his worst fears of being confined and remade. Restrain any impulse to pile it on. If your man agrees to eat slower, don't assume that while you're at it, you can heap on more suggestions regarding his manners. He has probably reached his limit with your first. (This isn't all male psychology, by the way. You feel the same.)

And be careful not to convey that he had no idea what he was doing before he met you . If you want your man to keep coming to you for ideas, he has to feel that his past won't be held against him. Your man wants to feel that he came into your life as a hero, not that he needs you or any woman to teach him how to behave.

LOYALTY NEEDS DURING A DISPUTE

Even during a heated dispute, loyalty is essential—and possible. Make strong statements if you wish, but stay fair. Never enter the **Territory of Disloyalty.** Of all the ways that you can hurt yourself in an argument, the worst (and sometimes the most inviting) is to enter that forbidden land. If you do, long after the issue is forgotten, your man will remember that you betrayed him, and he won't trust you again.

As we've seen, the most usual form of disloyalty during an argument is enlisting other people to support you. Your aim, when you do this, is to evoke an army on your side so that your man will *have* to see that he was in the wrong.

For example, say you are furious with your man because he often gives you things to do at the last minute, and doesn't live up to his own obligations. Yesterday he called at four o'clock and told you to pick up his mother at the airport. He had planned to meet her but calls you on his cell phone, saying that something just came up and he can't. You could conceivably have refused, or at least protested later on, but you did neither. Instead you choose a time to complain when you'll have witnesses and get support.

Two days later, at dinner, you turn to his brother's wife and ask, "Does your husband call you at the last minute and tell you to pick up your mother-in-law at the airport, or am I the only one who gets this kind of assignment?"

You may think that your witnesses are a plus for you—that they will help you convince your man that he did something wrong and unfair. But whether the witnesses agree with you or not is insignificant alongside the fact that you are humiliating your man. Your disloyalty in going public will escalate what was just a difference of opinion into a hopeless feeling on his part about the whole relationship. From your point of view, you were only soliciting help in making your case. But from his, you have put winning an argument above his feelings. You have shamed him publicly and assaulted his Masculine Pretense.

As I've mentioned, quoting your friends to your man while arguing with him is also a bad idea. He'll experience this negative talk about him as a betrayal every bit as serious as if you had attacked him in public. In a sense, it's worse than arguing in public because at least if he were there, he could have told his side of the story. This way, he's had no chance to say anything on his own behalf.

Sometimes you will need to start an argument *because* you are loyal to your man. No one wants to marry the school monitor, but if you can see big trouble ahead unless your man changes his course, loyalty demands that you say something. Even if your observation is unwelcome, you owe it to your man and to yourself to speak up if you see him doing something truly self-destructive.

Many a man who at first resented the woman he loved for a strong suggestion has been very appreciative later on. The woman who tells her guy that he has a drinking problem is sure to elicit great resentment at first. But later, after the incipient alcoholic gives up liquor entirely and sees his life turn around, he is deeply thankful to her for her caring and for the guts to help him avoid throwing away his life.

You know the difference between a courageous remark made out of loyalty and a carping criticism that you make in annoyance. It's one thing to nag your man to quit a life-threatening habit, like smoking, and another to batter him for getting up late on weekends.

In many cases, the problem is that the man is carrying psychological baggage. We all carry a certain amount of extra baggage that weighs us down. In a relationship, this load burdens the team and not just the individual. Sometimes loyalty consists of helping your man to get rid of his emotional overload and travel much lighter than he ever did. Be sure to pick your spots carefully. But if you are sure you're right, you owe him your opinion even if it results in an argument. It may be worth it for both of you.

*   *   *

Kelli, a patient of mine, watched her boyfriend, Mark, constantly taken advantage of by Gene, an old friend of his. She loved Mark for his generosity but felt sure that this wasn't simply an instance of pure generosity on his part. He was afraid to say no.

Gene would regularly ask Mark for lifts, borrow equipment and forget to return it, and come over at all hours for advice about his job. There was plenty to talk about, since Gene lost one job after another. Kelli felt sure that Mark sensed that he was being misused but didn't want to admit this even to himself. Once when Mark asked Gene for a favor, Gene turned him down, and Mark looked crushed. But that night, when Kelli expressed anger toward Gene, Mark instantly defended him. "Oh, he's just having a bad time right now. That's all."

Kelli came into my office with a written list of favors that Mark had done for Gene. It included some that Mark had prevailed on her to take care of, for which she had never been thanked by Gene. By then she hated Gene and was angry with Mark, though she also loved him very much.

I told her to throw the list away. Lists never help in arguments. If anything, they make other people determined to defend their behavior as a way of explaining why they have been so consistent. I suspected that Mark would do this, perhaps by citing Gene's plight, and possibly by calling Kelli unsympathetic.

But I did help Kelli make her point. We decided that the next time Gene wanted something from him, Kelli would ask Mark to refuse it on the grounds that if Gene were a real friend, he would understand.

Gene still owed Mark fifteen hundred dollars, but within a month asked to borrow two hundred more. At first Mark wanted to rush the money over. (He would typically deliver it himself to save Gene the time.)

Kelli was ready. "Please don't. Won't he still love you if you turn him down?" Kelli asked. When Mark assured her that of course Gene would, Kelli said, "Okay, then prove it."

Hard as it was for Mark, he put Gene to the test. Gene got furious. He accused Mark of deserting him just when it really counted.

Mark was stunned at Gene's reply, and even more stunned when Gene didn't return his phone calls a week later. "I thought this was a real friendship," Mark said. "I guess I just didn't want to see that it wasn't."

By staying specific and not making a sweeping generalization about Gene (or about Mark, for that matter), Kelli got her point across effectively. She won the argument, but at the same time she let Mark feel special. She underscored her loyalty to him by showing how much she was on his side.

Kelli's intervention, which troubled Mark at first, actually enabled him to travel lighter than he had before he met her, by freeing him of this burdensome person in his life. The ideal arguments between lovers will often lead to this kind of positive result.

PRESERVING INTIMACY WHILE ARGUING

Can you feel truly loving during a heated argument? Probably not. It would be a supreme act of denial to pretend that you're infatuated with a man while he's yelling at you. You certainly don't feel loved, and it's hard to remember that you ever loved him. But you know how quickly feelings change. Very likely, you will be intimate again—as long as you can both avoid saying or doing anything seriously destructive.

This is because your intimacy isn't just a momentary feeling. It's a *relationship* that the two of you built over time together—when you were happy, when you shared tender moments, and under stress when you both pitched in toward a common goal. Intimacy is a city that you dwelled in together, with edifices for work, for sex, for recreation, and for future planning. This city still stands, despite the clouds that obscure it during a heated argument. The important thing is to leave the city intact so that the two of you can return to it.

The various suggestions I've already made in this chapter will help you to avoid doing long-term damage to the intimacy you've established, even during those moments when it is hard to picture a future together. Remember what an argument is, and what it is not. You are trying to make a point, not inflict punishment.

Intimacy depends on trust. As we've seen, your man can give you this trust only when he's convinced that you'll stay loyal to him and see his specialness even in tough times. If you want your relationship to remain standing, try not to say things simply to get your man's attention by inflicting pain. No matter how angry or hurt you feel, don't fight dirty, because that would be saying exactly what you should never say: "My love is *conditional*, and if you cross me, all bets are off, and you had better watch out." If you convey this, then long after the argument, the injury to your intimacy will remain, and this faulty foundation of your romance will be hard to repair.

The two most common lapses into dirty fighting that do much more injury than the offender reckons are *sarcasm* and *sexual insults*. Avoid them both.

The only purpose of sarcasm is to hurt the guy. Sarcastic comments are always made to ridicule the other person and show that his flaws are glaring and laughable. "I can see why your ex-girlfriend dumped you. To someone with a big job like hers, you must have really looked brain damaged." "I'd ask you to help me set the table, but they probably didn't do that in your house."

Sarcastic comments may be fun for you to make. But is it worth it to entertain yourself at the risk of ruining your relationship? These comments have a way of resonating in the other person's mind, whether you want them to or not. Once you tell your man that you see something ugly about him, you can't just take it back. The next day it would be hard to convince the guy that you don't see him as incompetent or his family as a bunch of slobs.

Even more resonating to your man are *sexual insults*. As we've seen, being a good lover is critical to your man's sense of self. Comments made in anger about your man's premature ejaculations, or his failure to get an erection, or his sexual awkwardness will remain in the atmosphere and poison it long after this argument is over.

Some years ago, a couple sat in my office at far ends of the couch, not looking at each other. The woman talked first and said that they'd had a great sexual relationship until a big argument about a month ago. After it, the man had pulled back sharply. He was still pleasant to her and saw her as often. But his enthusiasm was evidently gone.

When she asked him what went wrong, he didn't respond, but it became clear that he had something in mind, that she'd made some comment to him that he couldn't or wouldn't let go of. Later, after we virtually begged him to tell us what it was, he did. During an argument, she'd commented that her previous boyfriends had been tall and muscular; he was neither. She had used the unfortunate phrase "You're not really my type."

Her attempted amendment in my office—"But I love you, and I never loved any of them"—fell on deaf ears. Every man needs to see himself as exactly the lover that his woman has wanted to be with. Grandiose? Of course. But it is an integral part of the Masculine Pretense. She had doubtless spoken with a momentary desire to inflict pain, but her malicious comment struck home more devastatingly than she had bargained for. They broke up soon afterward.

Your man is especially vulnerable to sexual insults because his sexuality is part of his personal myth. But attacks on *any* part of your man's myth will inflict similar damage. Just as you built intimacy by respecting his personal myth, you risk destroying it by slashing at that myth. Ironically, it is during an argument that you may want to use your special intelligence about your man to strike at his most vulnerable point. Since you now know what it is and how sensitive he is about it, it may look like an easy target. But don't fire at that target if you want the relationship to live after the argument is over.

No matter how angry you get, never slash at your man's personal myth, his vitally important vision of himself and what he could be. Over time, you have gotten to know what your man treasures about himself—for instance, that even though he has gotten divorced, he has always been loving and protective toward his son. True, you'll get his attention with a comment like: "You're controlling with me, just the way you're controlling with your kid. That's why he always has to run to his mother if he wants to be heard." It's a showstopper. But long after the dispute is over, your man will remember it. Is this what you really think? Does he really want to marry a woman who feels that he mistreats his son and that he'll mistreat her in the same way? He has a new and hard question to consider. You would be far better off having left his son out of this dispute.

If your man loves you and is considering marriage, he needs to know that you regard him as a loving father, a loving *person*, even though he screws up here and there. Stay loyal to your man's personal myth, and your dispute with him will remain local instead of poisoning his mind afterward.

Remember the first rule of arguing. Allow your man to go on liking himself, even while you are contesting him on some point. If he treasures something about himself, why would he want to spend his life with a woman who calls that picture of his into question?

SEX AFTER AN ARGUMENT

We all know how good sex can be after a fierce argument with a lover. The closer you came to breaking up, the better it can be. During the clash you imagined losing him, being all alone again, explaining your failed romance to friends. You were desolate. Now here he is back, loving you. Sex bridges the great gulf that was between you and gives the romance a brand-new feeling. It's exciting, and his passion seems to say that all is well again. Sex before was good, but this experience is special.

But be sure that you aren't using sex as a form of persuasion—to get him to do something for you or to see things your way. For instance, maybe you argued with him about what you considered a flirtation with another woman, which your man is continuing. Your man called you paranoid and questioned whether he'd have any freedom at all if he married you. This heated exchange was very painful for both of you, and pushed you miles apart in minutes. He's angry, so you make an overture, and get sex started. Afterward, your man isn't angry with you anymore. But though sex has terminated the argument, it hasn't solved anything. You still feel endangered by his flirtations, and he worries that he can never travel light with you if he signs up.

The whole purpose of the discussion was to *air* your differences, but you used sex to suppress them instead. Because the discussion was cut off, you are both left with a general hopelessness about the romance. Even if the sex was great, it severed communication, and you will both sense that you've just put off dealing with the problem.

Women patients sometimes tell me that the best sex they ever had was in a stormy relationship that couldn't last. For a time, they fell into a pattern. They would fight with the man, have great sex, go along quietly for a while, and then start over. Once again, they would fight to the point of nearly breaking up, would use sex to blur the issue, and nothing would really improve. Their arguments were an aphrodisiac, but the root problems never got solved, and they finally broke up.

The bottom line is: finish your discussion first. Resolve your differences, if you can, *before* you make love. If you don't, what you bury will come back to haunt you later.

SEALING OVER THE ARGUMENT

A key to arguing is having the sense to know when the argument is over. When it is, let it go. You've made your point once or twice, if not more. He has responded, and you've gone back and forth a few times. Usually, someone will seem to be winning. Either he has seen your point, or right now you just can't get through. None of this has been very orderly, of course. You've probably both overstated your case, and you've certainly interrupted each other plenty. But you've accomplished as much as you can for now.

If you're the one who is winning, don't keep banging at your man until he gives you a signed confession. You won't get one, and that shouldn't be your aim. Most men, because of their Masculine Pretense, find it hard to apologize outright. But this doesn't mean your man fails to see the light.

If you don't feel as if you're winning, there's no point in pressing until one of you says something unforgivable. Leave the issue alone for now. If your man cares for you, he may think it over and come around when he doesn't feel challenged.

Many a dispute has been won—the other person grudgingly recognizes the truth of an argument—only to be lost by repetition. Overkill has ruined as many relationships as not speaking up at all. Letting a dispute go proves that your aim has been to make a point and not to pound your man into submission or to make him feel guilty. Ending an argument without referring to it or brooding about it afterward is a real show of intimacy.

Arguing may be unpleasant, but it's an expression of hope that the two of you together can remedy problems in your romance. If a woman friend tells you, "My man and I never argue," she is probably lying. And that's the best scenario. If she's telling the truth, at least one of the partners must feel totally hopeless and has settled for doing exactly what the other person wants. Shakespeare wrote that "the course of true love never did run smooth." Basically, the art of arguing is to ask for what you want and complain if you must, but without going beyond the particular issue, so that afterward your relationship remains standing and is stronger than ever.

9

When There's Big Trouble

ARE YOU GIVING TOO MUCH?

Though this book has mainly emphasized your man's needs, my intention has not been for you to sacrifice yourself unduly. In fact, learning your man's needs is a way of getting him to fulfil yours. The key word is *balance*. Men are quick to feel neglected. Because of their Masculine Pretense, it may be hard to see this, and we've been studying your man's needs so that you will understand what your man probably can't put into words.

But sometimes you'll find that you've been tipping the balance too far in your man's direction and neglecting yourself. Now you are the one feeling unhappy and unfulfilled. The time has come to recognize this and rectify the balance.

Let's say that you have argued with him, and you've actually won many of your points, but you still feel terrible. You've come to resent the fact that everything has to be an argument, and these days you often feel like fighting with him for no reason at all. Or maybe it's even worse. You're sick of arguing. You've lost your impulse to try to get through; it seems pointless. Besides, you can no longer single out any one thing he's doing that would make a real difference. You'd really like him to change everything.

When you start feeling this way, obviously there's deep trouble in the relationship. Whatever is really bothering you goes beyond what a single argument can address or solve. There's an imbalance that is causing you a lot of pain. This imbalance may be a trend that you feel is taking over, and you hate it. You do all the unpleasant chores. You are the one who always gives in when there's a dispute. His dream always matters more than yours. Or maybe there's some trait of his that you thought would soften, but it's only gotten worse. He never admits that he's wrong about even the smallest thing. Or you're always the one who has to apologize.

Maybe he has begun to act as if everything that matters to you is trivial. He doesn't focus on your concerns the way you focus on his. If asked, he might not even be able to say what you want most in life, what you're most afraid of, or why you like the people you do. As a result, you are losing touch with your own dreams, your own ambitions, the things that always mattered so much to you.

It's as if you shifted the great spotlight of your unconscious, which always guided you, and shined it on him. Now you're feeling somewhat confused and lost. This all amounts to big trouble.

In moments of clarity, maybe after a few drinks with friends, or just before you go to sleep at night, or in those morning moments when you are alone sipping a cup of coffee, you have clear glimpses of what the problem is. In those interludes, you could define it precisely to anyone who cared to ask you about it. But usually, you push it away. You deny the problem and its magnitude.

Most of the time, you feel that you can't solve this amorphous problem without ending the relationship. With a sense of futility, you say to yourself, "If his dreams are more important than mine, maybe that's the way it should be."

*   *   *

Obviously, every relationship is different. But real trouble in a romance will always show itself by your experiencing any—or all—of the following three symptoms:

1. **Having chronic anger.** You are annoyed at him continually. You are almost like a burn victim when he touches you relating to any subject where you disagree. When you have an argument, you don't really want to restrict it to a single point. You'd like to bring in his entire history, go for the jugular, and tear this man to shreds.

2. **Being full of self-criticism.** Anything that troubled you in the past about yourself seems worse now. You feel too old, too fat, not educated enough, not number one in your field, you need a face-lift. Supply your own faults; they all seem glaring.

3. **Feeling a general loss of interest.** You have little desire to see your close friends. Hobbies that mattered to you don't matter anymore. You've lost sight of goals. You are going limp, doing what your man wants, but listlessly. This is a form of depression.

When you are in this mire, you are living a self-fulfilling prophecy. You feel too broken to do anything. As things get worse and worse, you feel even more helpless. Although this sorry relationship no longer resembles what you once wanted, it may now seem like the best you can do. It feels like what you deserve. The danger is that as you come to feel powerless, you start to convince yourself that this is the way things *have* to be. "Okay, I'll give him all the attention. When he criticizes me, he is probably right. I *should* spend more time at the gym. I *am* getting old."

But going limp is the worst thing you can do. You need to rally yourself enough to realize that you have reached a critical place in your relationship. You have followed all the rules and tried to fulfill his needs, but you have followed them too far and too well.

Nearly all big trouble in love relationships comes when one of the partners is giving too much. The bad trend in the relationship is that you are bending yourself out of shape. This is why you are having your symptoms.

Is there still hope for the romance? Is it him or is it you? Is this a guy who has to be in control and won't allow a fair balance? Or are you just unnecessarily compliant? Has fulfilling his needs led you to put them above your own?

If he's the problem, you'll discover this by a simple trial that we'll be talking about soon. There are certain men who are so limited by their Masculine Pretense that they won't allow a woman real breathing room. They insist on having things *their way*—their Masculine Pretense makes them unfair and unyielding. If your man *is* this way, then you may have already recognized this consciously or unconsciously. You have evolved your style of compliance to cope with him, and now your self-esteem is starting to break down, making it harder and harder for you to go on.

But in most cases, women who give too much are only imagining that their man is tougher than he is. Your man has blustered and been brittle and flashed his Masculine Pretense. You have bought his act too uncritically. Unlike those women who stood up to their man early on, when it was a matter of their dignity, you caved in on every single issue, and now you are suffering.

You have your own reasons for not having spoken up. Maybe because of the last guy you were with, or because of what you learned to expect from men as a child, you now cater to men as a matter of routine. Or you've convinced yourself that you want a relationship so badly that it doesn't matter how this man treats you. Whatever the reason, if it has been *your choice* to give too much, then there is hope. You can save this romance.

But to do this, you will have to diagnose yourself and the relationship. To save this romance, if you still can, you have to understand precisely what giving too much really means.

WHEN ARE YOU GIVING TOO MUCH?

Giving too much isn't a matter of quantity. One of you may contribute much more money, spend longer hours working, do all the initiating of sex, do nearly all the social planning for the team. But none of this implies automatically that the giver is giving too much.

The only real indication of whether you are giving too much is your motive. *Why* are you doing this? Is it voluntary? Can you *not* do it and feel just as secure in the relationship? Healthy giving is done with a sense that "I don't *have* to do this, but I *want* to." The mark of giving too much is a sense lurking in your motivation that "this is expected of me. I will be in big trouble if I *don't* do it."

Nothing that you do for your man, if your motive is kindness, or genuine desire, can ever be too much. And *anything* that you do for your man, if your motive is the *fear* "I had better do this, or else"— is too much.

You might spend three days preparing a dinner party for your man's newly married friend and his wife, or an afternoon bringing your man's parents back from the airport; it won't be too much if it's what you really want to do—if you feel that it isn't "required." You have the luxury of knowing that next time, if you're busy, you won't have to prepare the dinner or go to the airport, and no one will think less of you or pull back in any way.

So as long as you aren't being intimidated, the act won't hurt you, even if you aren't 100 percent in the mood.

Your man wants to make love tonight. You really don't. You're exhausted or just not feeling sexual. Still, you love the guy, and though you have an easy option to say no, you enjoy the closeness and you decide to have sex. Whether or not the experience takes off for you, you made a purely voluntary decision.

Contrast this with the scenario in which you are far from in the mood but know from past experience that if you say no, this guy will be hurt and furious, and things won't be the same. You have sex with him to avoid punishment. This time, because your motive is really *fear of displeasing your man*, you are giving too much.

Of course we all give too much at times, even to those we love. No single act of giving too much will be decisive or do serious harm to you or the relationship. It's the *pattern* of giving too much, the quiet acceptance of giving too much to your man in order to keep him, that produces the symptoms—your chronic anger, your self-criticism, or your loss of interest in activities and in life itself.

Once you fall into this pattern, it's very hard to see that this single relationship with this individual has been the cause. The transition from feeling proud of yourself, attractive and young, to feeling old and hopeless can occur within months. If you thought about it rationally, you would see that you started getting down on yourself only when you became seriously involved with this man. But right now you aren't rational, and you feel as if you suddenly crossed an age threshold or are finally seeing yourself realistically, and it isn't good.

Katie, a nurse, was thirty-two but considered herself old. She was amazed and gratified when the psychiatrist in charge of the hospital floor she worked on asked her out on a date. A relationship developed quickly. Later, she would tell me, "He's not like my previous boyfriends. He's incredibly sane. And he helps people every day."

It didn't seem like much of a sacrifice to Katie to let her hair grow long because Rob insisted on it, though it was a lot of trouble and she didn't think she looked nearly as good. She tried to read more serious literature because Rob made fun of those "trashy" novels she enjoyed. She saw less of her friends, whom he considered trivial, and when Rob spoke, she saw nearly everything he said as a wonderful new insight.

Katie knew that many other women in the hospital envied her for dating "Dr. Rob." When he gave her an engagement ring, she flashed it everywhere. It was a trophy procured by great sacrifice. Trying to please Rob and doing whatever he said seemed a natural continuation of Katie's role on "his" floor in the hospital, and of her early childhood, in which she had been a dutiful daughter.

The first real trouble came in the form of Katie's going dead sexually. She stopped having orgasms during intercourse and then stopped feeling anything at all. This seemed inexplicable because, according to Katie, "Dr. Rob" was a good lover who could "hold out a long time." However, he didn't believe in sexual consummation other than during intercourse; it was against his psychoanalytic principles.

Dr. Rob was very upset by Katie's nonresponse to him and told her that it was a serious defect. He attributed what he called her "frigidity" to childhood problems and recommended that she see a psychoanalytic colleague of his. But Katie put him off, and when a woman friend recommended me, she came to my office instead, without telling him.

As we talked, I could see that Katie had tried to give Rob everything, and in the process, had given him too much by far. By then, they had stopped discussing wedding dates. I could see that what appeared to be anesthesia in Katie was actually rebellion, which she was expressing sexually. Katie's complete nonresponsiveness was her way of saying what she lacked the courage to say in words—that she felt neglected and unloved, and was quitting the game. Her subconscious had told her to withhold from Dr. Rob what he wanted most, pride in himself as a lover. This was the nature of her reprisal against him. Katie's seeing me behind Dr. Rob's back was a more obvious form of revolt. As Katie told me about having great sex with several previous lovers, with no problems on either side, I felt surer than ever of my diagnosis.

Before long, Katie began to surface her negative feelings about Rob. No doubt he was too demanding. Still, she'd had choices along the way. She might have refused requests of his that she felt were unreasonable and unfair. They weren't sovereign demands, after all.

I asked Katie if she thought that Rob would leave her if she refused to let her hair grow out. "No, of course, not," she said. "It was just that he never stopped talking about how nice it would look." Katie had wanted to resist Rob on a dozen fronts, but she had chosen not to. She had not allowed herself to pinpoint her real options and thus made excessive sacrifices on the grounds that each was small.

Not long after we began working together, Katie reported having a violent argument with Rob in which all the rules were broken. Rob accused her of being "asexual"; she told him how good sex had been with other men, and she went on to blast Rob with numerous hostile observations that she'd made about him but had repressed as fast as she'd made them. Her fluency in dredging them up surprised Katie herself. After that, there seemed no turning back for either of them, the citadel had been destroyed, and they broke up soon afterward.

Everything that Katie had said was in a sense accurate. But like all women who give too much unquestioningly, the one thing that Katie didn't give her man was the chance to reconsider his requirements. Perhaps Rob would have been much more flexible if Katie had been outspoken along the way. We'll never know. On the assumption that Rob wouldn't have relented an inch but was a born tyrant, she had suppressed her wishes and allowed her rage eventually to grow out of all proportion.

> *I was angry with my friend:*
> *I told my wrath, my wrath did end.*
> *I was angry with my foe:*
> *I told it not, my wrath did grow.*

This formula, given to us two centuries ago by William Blake, still holds. The woman who gives too much is assuming that the man she loves is a foe, and the growth of her own rage, which then topples the relationship, is one of the bad endings that overgiving often leads to.

In her next relationship, Katie was careful to identify her own needs and not to let them fester, not to give too much. The following year, she connected with a great guy, and because she dealt with issues as they arose, she never saw him as overdemanding.

AFTEREFFECTS AS CLUES TO OVERGIVING

Naturally, you can't pinpoint your motives every time you do something for someone else. You can't always ask yourself, "Do I really want to do this or am I afraid not to?" Complicating matters is the fact that you'll often have mixed motives. Though you may want to do something, you also feel that you should.

Fortunately you have a "giving" test available that will help you figure out your motives most of the time. The test is to see how you feel *afterward*—after you have done the thing. If you really wanted to do the favor, then afterward you will feel happier, closer to your man, pleased with yourself, glad that you did it. Pure giving is a source of pleasure to the giver and brings the giver closer to the receiver.

On the other hand, if you did the thing because you felt that you *had* to, you won't feel better afterward. You'll feel worse. You won't feel closer to your man or better about yourself. You will feel weaker, more resigned to a worse life, and resentful. You'll feel that your man *made* you do the thing, even if he knew nothing about it.

Let's go back to the example of picking up your man's parents at the airport. If you like them and really wanted to greet them, you will feel happy after the chore. Even if it was a difficult ride and took a chunk out of your day, you will have a glow that says it was worthwhile. On the other hand, if you felt that your man *required* you to sacrifice your afternoon and didn't care what else you had to do, you will probably feel dismal afterward. You'll feel annoyed with his parents, and be depressed or experience a simmering anger toward your man.

Look at an act together with its aftereffect and you will get a good indication of why you acted and whether you did too much. Aftereffects never lie.

The trouble is that once a habit becomes chronic—after you've been giving your man too much for a while—it gets harder to view your emotional state as an aftereffect. But depression about a romance nearly always means that you've made too many compromises. So does the symptom of chronic rage. You wouldn't be so depressed or angry if you weren't making hurtful sacrifices and not doing enough of what *you* want.

Women who tell me that life has become pointless and that their romance is disappointing seldom see the real cause. Like Katie, they slowly developed a *habit of compliance* (either because it was demanded by the man or because they *thought* it was). They wanted to be sure that they didn't lose the guy, but they lost their zest for life and their self-esteem instead. By the time I saw them, they couldn't even imagine an easy, loving relationship. They certainly didn't see that *they* were doing anything that made their own lives harder.

The cure requires that you determine the ways in which you are giving too much. Where are you overdoing the theme of trying to make your man happy? If your relationship is faltering, there is one simple way to determine who is at fault. You'll find out the answer as you gradually stop catering to your man, first in small ways and then in bigger ones.

Let's study how your willingness to take the risk of disappointing your man here and there might set the whole relationship straight. If he's a decent guy, he will be glad that you are restoring your self-esteem and setting the relationship back in balance. He will prefer you as an equal. You will be a better companion if you are cheerful and positive, without doing the extra services, than depressed with having to provide them. If it turns out that he wants you only as a servant or that he enjoys treating you like a child, you'll have to move on. You may mourn his loss for weeks or months. And if you decide that he isn't the guy you thought he was, you may go through a period of doubting your own judgment. You may wonder how you could have gone so far with the wrong man. But these are small penalties to pay alongside that of spending the rest of your life unhappy and living in denial.

RECOVERING YOUR ROMANCE

Your aim is to get to the heart of the problem and recover this romance if it's worth it and possible. Don't waste time speculating about how your man really feels about you and whether there's any hope left. You've probably done too much of this already. If things have gone sour for a time, you really can't speculate anyway. You may be too full of self-doubt and your self-esteem may be too low to make a good evaluation, which is why you probably go in circles every day as you think about your relationship.

Instead of speculating, follow the steps that I am going to give you now. If you do, you are likely to restore your romance, and you will certainly restore your self-esteem. If he's the wrong guy, you'll find this out too. Remarkably, following these steps will tell you not just *where* you are overgiving but also *why*. As you follow them, you are going to learn the truth about this man, and also a great deal about yourself.

LIST YOUR SELF-DESTRUCTIVE SACRIFICES

Your first task is to simply *identify* things you do for your man that make you unhappy or that you quietly resent. Get a pad or start a new file on your computer, and write down as many of these acts of catering as possible. You are going to spend *two weeks* listing these suspicious acts, which make you feel as if you're constantly bailing out a boat that may be sinking. You won't remember every single thing, and you'll add items as you go along, but two weeks' worth will be a good start.

Thinking in terms of certain categories will help you find those places where you are giving too much. One such category might be chores that you do alone. You somehow end up doing all the trash work. He never volunteers for anything around the house, and you're starting to feel demeaned, as if he's a prince and you're the scullery maid. Or maybe you make all the social plans and you're starting to hate yourself because he isn't appreciative and he never comes up with an idea. Without you, Thanksgiving would be just another Thursday and weekends would be a time to sleep. It may be even worse if when you suggest that he pitch in, he tells you that the thing you want is *your* idea, not *his*. "I wouldn't make a big deal about Thanksgiving on my own. I don't care about cooking. You're the one who wants it." Or, "I don't obsess about having a neat apartment. You're the one who's picky, so leave me out of it."

It's probably easier than you thought to list things that you do alone that feel unfair because he doesn't pitch in. Write them down, one item on a line.

Also include in your list (of behaviors that you are going to change) the fact that you're not talking about things that matter to you, topics that you *want* to talk about, but which he doesn't. He talks on and on about *his* subjects: his work, his favorite baseball team, his mother, his friends. But when you try to discuss your interests, he has limited attention. He suggests that your topics are trivial, and you go along with this. You drop your subject, or don't bring it up at all, so as not to offend him. Add to your list these decisions to stay quiet. They amount to the choice to subordinate yourself.

Still another category of overgiving is holding still for mistreatment of certain kinds. Your man criticizes you regularly, or he's snide, or cynical, either when you're alone or with friends. You have been *choosing* to allow this—choosing not to speak up, at least not very decisively. You have been afraid that your man might get annoyed or upset with you.

Maybe you let it pass when he said in front of friends that you had no money sense. Or you held your breath in silence when he implied that you were overweight. You know that his last two girlfriends were anorexic, but still you took it hard. You have been blaming yourself instead of questioning his standard for how a woman should look. Whatever the form of injury, you've tried to tell yourself that he's been having tough times at work or that he doesn't really mean what he says. But you felt stung each time, and now you see that you have made a succession of choices *not* to say anything, even when you've felt hurt. Write these choices down too.

Add to your list things that you yourself have quit doing because your man doesn't want you to but that really are quite reasonable or important for you to do. Your man is jealous when you spend time on the phone with friends at night, so now you brush people off in order not to anger him. When you do make a fifteen-minute call, you make it surreptitiously. You have been making choices of this kind too, invisible but significant ones: decisions to *forgo* activities.

Your items will be highly subjective, of course. No one else would compile the exact list that you will. Among the unnecessary compromises you personally are making, some are acts that would be fine for many other women. It's just that they go against the grain of who you really are and want to be. You aren't trying to be someone else, you are trying to be yourself. So put down these items too.

For instance, one woman I worked with realized that her boyfriend of six months was trying to get her to live like a trophy wife. He expected her to look devastating every minute of the day, even on Saturday mornings when she went out to do neighborhood chores. In recent months "against her will," she was spending considerable time arraying herself before going out to buy a container of milk. To this woman it looked like treason to defy her boyfriend and pick up her cleaning in a jogging suit.

For another woman I treated the problem was the opposite. This woman *enjoyed* dressing up and looking her best at all times. She used to joke that she hadn't left the house without full makeup since she was fourteen. Her man thought that this was silly and time-consuming. Disregarding her preference, he often made last-minute plans for the two of them to meet friends, leaving my patient insufficient time to fix herself up the way she wanted to. She ended up spending uncomfortable evenings envying the other women who'd had more time to put themselves together. For this woman, the necessary "treason" was to demand all the preparation time she needed. If her man proved selfish enough not to give her this time, she planned not to be ready, thus making her point.

Both women had been catering to their man, and both were suffering as a result. They had "opposite" items on their lists, but both items were valid. Both women needed to change, and they each had a right to do what made them happy.

RANK THE ITEMS ON YOUR LIST

Study your list. Maybe you've found twenty acts of overgiving. Ask yourself what would happen if you simply pulled back? Suppose you said, "I'm not going to do this chore alone anymore. I'll insist that he help me." Or, "The next time he insults me in front of friends, I'm going to say something." Or, "The evening is the only time when I can talk to friends, so I'm going to call my friend Hillary tonight and hear everything about her new job, whether he likes it or not." When you contemplate changing items on your list, some of them will seem easier to change than others.

Rank the suspect behaviors on your list from 1 to 4. The number 1 means that you think that you can change the behavior fairly easily. The behaviors that get a 3 or 4 might feel to you like outright treason right now, and you are not going to attempt them as yet. Spend at least a week ranking these items, during which you will become even more familiar with them—and with your problem. Don't do any serious changing as yet. The more items on your list and the more accurately you have ranked them in order of difficulty, the easier it will be to change them.

CLIMBING THE LADDER

Start by making the simplest changes, those that you numbered 1. You may find, to your surprise, that a few that you put in this "easy" category seem almost impossible. You underestimated how hard they would be. When you made your list, it seemed easy to tell your man that he'd have to help you wait on friends when they came over. But once he's sitting on the couch in the middle of a conversation, you get cold feet about pulling him out to the kitchen. So you spend the whole evening filling people's glasses, passing out food, and feeling left out. When you wrote down "Get Aaron to help with guests," you thought that you were about to pick up a one-pound weight, but now you see that it's really a thirty pounder. No problem. Give the item a higher number. You will get to it later. It will become easier once you have gained strength and clarity by making the changes that you can handle now.

On the other hand, very likely you will want to reclassify a few of the higher number items into category 1. You thought that it would be nearly impossible to tell your man that his ex-wife has to get people other than him to do work around her house. Her demands are much too disruptive. But as you think about it, it irritates you increasingly, and you feel unexpectedly ready to say this. Go ahead and say it.

As you start climbing the ladder of these adjustments, you can't fail to see what's really going on. In the worst-case scenario, your man will be completely intolerant of your wishes. He'll tell you that his relationship with his ex-wife is none of your business. Or he'll get angry when you ask him to pitch in, even one percent. "If you don't feel like serving people when they come over for the Super Bowl, then don't. My friends can go get beers out of the refrigerator." The thought of twenty guys roaming through your kitchen (if they can find the kitchen) and rifling through your cabinets is horrifying. But your man has laid down the battle lines: he has told you to pass out the food and drink or suffer the consequences.

This is the *worst* possible outcome. What you feared proves true. The guy has none of your interests at heart. He can't give up any control, and he doesn't play well with other children—especially females. You have discovered that he doesn't consider the relationship worth his making any compromises. This may be why he's still single.

But his reformation or growth are not your project. Others have probably tried and failed, and they are better off not being with him anymore. You are *not* a failure, and certainly not responsible for his disastrous inability to love. It's a big temptation for a woman to try to turn an unloving man into one who can love and does love her. But, assuming that you have attended to your man's basic needs, you have done all that you can do. Rather than turn your life over to a fruitless venture, repeatedly blaming yourself for another person's limitations, your only recourse may be to end it and start with someone else.

Ninety percent of the time, however, this won't be the outcome. Many men will simply take your new behavior in stride. You'll be stunned to find out that what you feared was almost completely in your mind. When you ask your man to contribute, he agrees to, with a shrug and a "whatever." When you tell him you're going to spend Saturday antiquing with a close woman friend, he goes along with it. He's got plenty to do himself.

The majority of men are somewhere in the middle, or this book wouldn't be necessary. Your man's Masculine Pretense will leave him feeling a bit wounded when he feels opposed. He may look askance and try to persuade you to cater to him more than you really want to. "Can't you go antiquing with Beth when I'm out of town on business?" Or, "Can we really afford to buy antiques right now?" Or, a hangdog look, followed by, "I was really looking forward to . . ."

"You'll feel misgivings or a pang of guilt, because he wants you to. But the serious consequences of letting him down, which you anticipated, are nowhere in sight. **Hold to your position,** and your man will soon get over whatever is bothering him. You will be happier, and get over your depression or anger. And your good cheer will make him happier with you. You are developing a reciprocal relationship, which creates a context for marriage, rather than sustaining a catering relationship, which does not.

As you devote yourself to the items in category 1, pay no attention to the other rungs of the ladder. Your first changes won't be easy, but you need to start somewhere to restore your self-esteem and make a real romance possible. Stay steadfast. Ignore it if your man acts mildly surprised at our nonconformity. You can keep his basic needs in mind without surrendering your own. Remember that if there is love on both sides, you are nurturing this love by being your best self once again.

You will have to spend about five weeks on each rung of the ladder, and you'll need some time afterward to patrol your behavior so that you don't lapse. But you will start to see gains early.

Marcy had watched her romance go downhill during the four months that she'd been living with Jonathan. They had been together for about a year, and now the bubbles were gone. As she discussed the relationship with me, Marcy realized that she had a gnawing fear of displeasing Jonathan in any way.

Jonathan had intrigued Marcy partly because he was a successful executive with a commanding style. He was used to having his own way. He wielded a lot of influence in the office, and he expected those in his personal life to comply with his wishes, almost as if they were staff. He would comment quickly when workmen or clerks in stores didn't serve him fast enough, and everyone close to him, including Marcy, felt in danger of his anger or disappointment if they didn't perform to his expectations.

Jonathan was very loving toward Marcy. He was often complimentary and was thoughtful about surprising her with little gifts and remembering special dates. Because she felt that he was a prize, it was extremely hard for her to disappoint him. Yet Jonathan was often disappointed, or at least he acted that way. Marcy could tell because he would raise a fastidious eyebrow when she didn't do quite what he expected.

Could the right woman loosen him up a bit? In Marcy, Jonathan had found a woman who was afraid to test that hypothesis. Marcy was trying to hard too comply with Jonathan's expectations, even unspoken ones, which she could surmise from that raised eyebrow or a mild word of disapproval.

When I suggested to Marcy that she make a list of how she might be overextending herself, she was at first resistant. I told her, however, that among the benefits of changing her behavior was that she would find out how serious about her Jonathan really was.

Among the items that Marcy set for herself as first challenges was to stop accounting for every minute of her time, as she had been. Before she had met Jonathan, Marcy had always looked forward to taking a bike ride after work. Now that she was with Jonathan, she still took her bike rides, but she always felt guilty. Every single night, Jonathan would ask her, "How long will you be?" She would make the time as short as she could—"A half hour. Okay?" She would be slightly anxious setting out, and after abbreviating her route, would experience a mild panic at the end and would hurry back in fear of being late.

Marcy's first symbolic self-assertion was to make sure that she returned at least ten minutes *after* the time Jonathan expected her. Though she knew that there was no real pressure—they had nowhere to go that evening—Marcy was surprised at the amount of fear she felt as those extra minutes ticked away. Only someone who has fought the problem of overconforming in a romance can appreciate how hard it was for Marcy to force herself to be late. She pictured Jonathan turning against her and remaining angry all evening. She even had flash visions of his not being in the apartment when she returned and calling her to say that the relationship was over.

In reality, Jonathan did flash her a look of annoyance. For the first time, Marcy felt angry at that look—she saw it as petty and critical in spirit, but still she wilted and immediately apologized for her "lateness." The next week, we added to her list not apologizing when she had done nothing wrong. That, too, was hard for Marcy, and she saw for the first time how often she found herself apologizing to Jonathan.

As she took better care of herself and, among other things, stopped scrutinizing Jonathan's facial expressions, Marcy's fear of "civil disobedience" subsided. Jonathan really did love her and was able to give up a power he should never have possessed in the first place.

Marcy realized that Jonathan had remained single in large part because of his excessive need to be in control. Before Marcy, and at first in Marcy herself, he had unconsciously selected women who would be subservient. In his previous two serious relationships, he and the woman had paid the price. Both women had catered to him unduly. They had lost their sense of their own attractiveness, grown resentful and depressed, and the relationships had died. In Marcy, Jonathan had finally found a woman who refused to give up her own identity, even in small ways. In the end, she had much more to offer to herself and to Jonathan than those who had thrown themselves away for him.

By completing the revisions on the first rung of her ladder, Marcy had built the confidence and given herself the perspective that brought the next rung of changes within range. She attacked each rung successively, did quite well, and in the process raised her self-esteem and her desirability still further.

Marcy saved the relationship by restoring parity. Though not all men truly want a woman they can respect (and some relationships just don't work out), I have found that most men do want a real partner. In spite of their Masculine Pretense, they are able to love and respect the right woman. Jonathan fell in love again with the old Marcy, and the two got married the following year.

SELF-DISCOVERY AS YOU IMPROVE YOUR ROMANCE

You've decided to study your overgiving in order to save your romance. But as a therapist, I can assure you that any study of yourself brings additional benefits. While climbing the ladder of personal change, you can discover a great deal about yourself. You can figure out *why* you have been overgiving—not just the obvious reasons (that you want to be married and don't want to be alone), but very deep reasons.

During those moments when you try risky, new behavior, you can get spectacular glimpses into yourself, even into your past. **You can actually identify fears that go way back to your childhood.**

To achieve this knowledge, don't dismiss your fear. Instead, look at it closely. Examine it, because it has a great deal to tell you that can help you in the future.

When Marcy told me her fantasy that Jonathan would be furious and might even *leave her* for her "defiance" in being late, she added quickly, "I knew better, but that's how it felt." Why this particular form of fantasy? I wondered, and asked Marcy, "Was there anyone in your early life whom you were afraid to disappoint, who you feared would abandon you?" She answered at once, "My father. He was always talking about 'team players' and how hurt he was when people let him down. Sometimes he wouldn't talk to my brother or me for days at a time."

Suddenly Marcy's fearful picture made sense. Marcy's father did in reality abandon her and her brother at a moment's notice when they displeased him. One minute he was a loving father, the next, he was a stranger who wouldn't even speak to them because of something they had done. Marcy had existed with a lifelong sense that someone you love can suddenly turn away from you if you displease them even for a moment.

By deliberately making herself less obedient and studying her reaction, Marcy had finally exposed her own driving force. She was averting *paternal disappointment*. By defying Jonathan and studying her own reaction, Marcy fully understood for the first time what she was really afraid of. Her childhood dread of being abandoned flashed into her mind as clearly as if it were a movie.

It turned out that Jonathan, though finicky, wasn't punitive, and he truly loved her—which Marcy repeatedly discovered as she continued up the ladder of change. After a while, when those images of Jonathan feeling broken and leaving her came to mind, Marcy could recognize them as unrealistic products of her past.

Soon it was obvious to Marcy that she had no need to rush home from her bike rides. When she asserted her independence, Jonathan stopped trying to pin her down to a specific return time. He began arranging his own routine around Marcy's nightly rides. Soon Marcy was able to enjoy them without even thinking about getting into trouble.

But for Marcy, tackling harder tasks still produced those same fantasies of punishment. When, two months later, Marcy told a friend of Jonathan's that she didn't want to hear any more of his sexist jokes, a terrible ten seconds of silence followed. Marcy was stricken with the thought that finally she had, indeed, gone too far, that Jonathan would tell her he was leaving. By then, however, Marcy knew enough to distrust the image; she recognized its source. When another woman at the dinner table said that she also hated the guy's jokes, Jonathan himself took their side and told his buddy, "I'm always telling you to give them up. They're high school stuff."

You will be surprised at the discoveries that you make as you examine your own reactions after being more assertive. One woman I worked with cringed as the image flashed through her mind that her lover would smack her in the face if she objected to his selfishness. Her stepfather had slapped her brothers for talking back to him. Though he never hit the girls, my patient's highly solicitous behavior was motivated by fear of reprisal in this form. She had never consciously identified this fear until she evoked a vivid picture-image of it by an act of deliberate "disobedience." When she did, she immediately figured out where the image had come from. She was horrified that she had allowed herself to live with such a primitive fear. Knowing what she was really afraid of helped this woman a great deal. She reminded herself that she was a big girl among adults now, and that no one could strike her for anything. Soon she was taking care of herself and expressing her opinions much more freely.

Another woman had the horrible picture that she was murdering her boyfriend whenever she felt that she was displeasing him. As a girl, she and her sister had lived in fear of killing their father, whose heart problems subdued the household and kept it in strict conformity. By the way, her father was still alive.

You can discover more about yourself when you break a habitual pattern than in any other way. The very function of habits is to relieve us of having to think about why we're acting. When you break a habit, the original purpose comes hurtling back—in the form of fear. Why fear? Because you are suddenly on insecure footing. You aren't doing what you are accustomed to. It's important to know that your fear is usually a response to the past, preserved by the habit as if it were sealed in amber.

In the unfortunate case when your fear is more than just a response to the past, you'll see this too right away. Your boyfriend may turn out to be a bully who insists on taking over your life. He'll make this obvious because he'll punish you. Certainly, some men become insufferable and won't let up.

On one woman's fourth rung was defying her very jealous boyfriend by walking home from the office with a male colleague who lived in the same building complex. There was nothing roman-tic between them, but they often had cathartic talks about troubles at work. They got real insights from each other, and it would have been very awkward for the woman to make repeated excuses for not walking ten blocks with him when they were leaving the office at the same time.

Still, she anticipated that her jealous boyfriend would practically have a seizure if he found out that they took these regular walks. She turned out to be right. When she mentioned that she often walked home with Dan, "who is very helpful," her boyfriend became wildly accusatory. Hardly letting her speak, he rattled off a number of other acts of hers over the months to which he objected. Though he hadn't brought them up, he recalled them vividly, and they apparently still burned him. A few made borderline sense; the rest were astonishing and bespoke a feverish and controlling mind. There was no turning back for either of them.

This woman was glad that she had begun ascending her ladder of personal dignity because it had enabled her to see that she was with the wrong man. She took care of herself in the next relationship and ended what might have been a lifetime of cater-and-die love affairs.

Nearly always, though, as you commence taking care of yourself, you will find that you've been greatly exaggerating the penalties for setting the relationship right. As you see vividly what you've been afraid of, you will appreciate that to a large extent you have been afraid of a ghost. The guy you're with isn't an all-powerful father, or stepfather, or brother, or mother. He isn't your last boyfriend He's just a man trying to figure out what life and love are all about, not unlike you. And if he loves you, he certainly won't want to lose you.

10

Your Most Important Relationship

How can I be true?
Should I be faithful to myself or you?

The right answer to this question, framed in these words by the poet Sara Teasdale, is that, for a marriage to happen and to succeed, you have to be faithful to *both*. Even more important than your romance is your relationship with yourself. If you have to betray yourself to get this guy to marry you, he probably won't, and even if he does, you have created a big problem.

In this book, I have talked about your man's secret needs, and by now you probably know much more about them than he can put into words. His Masculine Pretense to some extent blinds him to his need to feel special, his need to travel light, his need for loyalty, and his need for intimacy. But the art of making a love affair work isn't simply to fulfill his needs: it is to fulfill your man while giving yourself what you need too.

If this book were about golf, or mathematics, or money, I probably wouldn't have to remind you: "Don't forget that your own self-esteem and fulfillment are more important than what we are talking about." But when it comes to love, it is sadly easy to forget your self-esteem, your needs, and even your childhood aspirations—the visions of a happy relationship that have kept you going through the ups and downs.

Your challenge, then, is to achieve a balance in which your man is fulfilled, but also one in which he appreciates your needs and wants to fulfill them too. This isn't as hard as it seems, if you know how. Most men want love and marriage, despite their constant joking that they don't, but when things don't work out "automatically," they tend to move on cynically, rather than do soul-searching and have serious discussions about what is going wrong. Your learning what your man is really like will give you access so that this doesn't happen. But you need to retain access to yourself also, and to convey those truths to him.

Marriage is more a marathon than a sprint, but it isn't a pure case of either. It's a marathon that begins with a sprint. If it is to work, you have to be comfortable with the pace that you set. You have to be yourself—your best self, if possible, but your true self. Too much subordination of self, by serving your man or by pretending to be what you are not, will make it impossible for you to run the marathon.

This is your challenge, but the reward is huge. While loving your man, don't forget yourself. The right guy wouldn't want you to. Any man worth anything, who loves you, will derive great satisfaction from making you happy. In fact, you will *know* that he's the right guy if you can love him and love yourself. Give yourself the chance, and give him the chance too.

ABOUT THE AUTHOR

George Weinberg, Ph.D., is a clinical psychologist and the author of nine books, including *Self Creation, The Heart of Psychotherapy,* and *Society and the Healthy Homosexual* (in which he coined the term "homophobia"). He has appeared on many national radio and television shows, including *The Oprah Winfrey Show* and *Live with Regis and Kathy Lee,* and has written frequently for magazines from *Cosmopolitan* and *Glamour* to *TV Guide* and *Reader's Digest.*